Ohio's Grand Canal

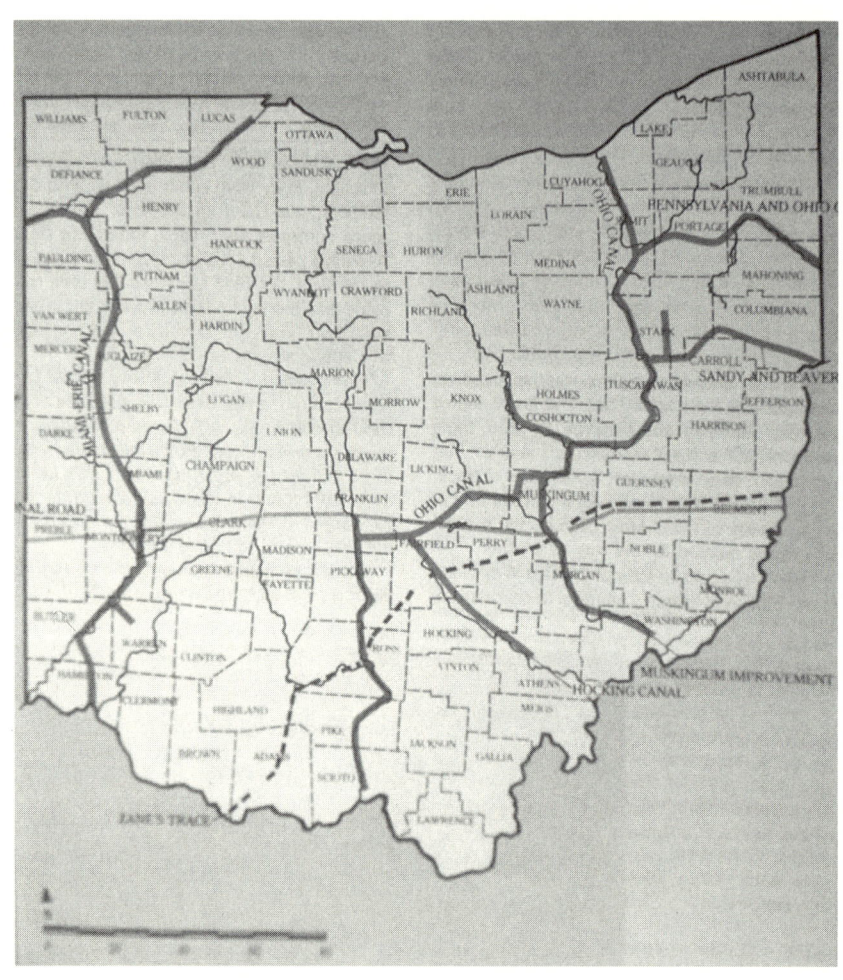

Map of Ohio showing all major canals.
(George W. Knepper, *Ohio and Its People*)

Ohio's Grand Canal

A Brief History of the
Ohio & Erie Canal

Terry K. Woods

The Kent State University Press
Kent, Ohio

© 2008 by The Kent State University Press, Kent, Ohio 44242
ALL RIGHTS RESERVED
Library of Congress Catalog Card Number 2008021292
ISBN 978-0-87338-984-6

Unless otherwise noted, images are from the author's collection or
the Canal Society of Ohio Archives.

Manufactured in the United States of America

Library of Congress Cataloging-in-Publication Data
Woods, Terry K., 1937–
Ohio's grand canal : a brief history of the Ohio & Erie Canal / Terry K. Woods
   p.   cm.
Includes bibliographical references and index.
ISBN 978-0-87338-984-6 (hardcover : alk. paper) ∞
1. Ohio and Erie Canal (Ohio)—History.   I. Title.
HE396.O33W66 2008
386'.4809771—dc22   2008021292

British Library Cataloging-in-Publication data are available.

12 11 10 09 08   5 4 3 2 1

This book is dedicated to my parents, Kenneth and Fanchon,

my wife, Rosanne, and our five children and eight grandchildren.

A large portion of the time spent during the last forty years researching

and preparing this book was taken from them.

Contents

☙ 1 ❧
Planning and Construction

The Beginning

The canals of Ohio, once the mainstay of the state's transportation system, shunted Ohio products out of the state and necessities for the good life in. In just a little more than twenty-five years, these artificial waterways—and the men and women who lived and worked on or near them—transformed the state of Ohio from an isolated frontier, where farmers were unable to afford to ship their harvests to market, into a prosperous and influential agricultural and industrial power.

As per the Greenville Treaty of 1795, the western boundary of the United States was drawn south from Lake Erie along the Cuyahoga and Tuscarawas Rivers before veering to the west. The Treaty of Fort Industry in 1805 pushed that boundary even farther west into Ohio. Now, floods of settlers rushed into the "new west," which included western Virginia, Kentucky, Ohio, and beyond.

The first thing these new settlers did upon arriving in Ohio was clear a tract of land, build a cabin, and plant crops. Then, a few short years later, they were confronted with the problem of how to get their produce to market. The roads of the day, particularly those through the mountains to the eastern markets, were impassable quagmires in the spring and axle-breaking obstacle courses during the rest of the year.

The rivers were a little better if a spring freshet could be caught just right. A farmer would work and plan for months. He would then load his surplus product on a homemade flatboat, wait for the spring rains to

1

raise the water high enough to cover most of the snags and rocks, and float down the Tuscarawas, perhaps, to the Muskingum and Ohio and finally out onto the broad Mississippi to New Orleans. There he would sell his cargo, break up the boat and sell the lumber, and then make the long journey back home—usually on foot.

The problem was that nearly everyone in the "West" went to New Orleans on the same freshets. They all tried to sell the same goods to the same buyers at the same time. Often a cargo would be left on the docks to rot for want of a buyer. And for those fortunate enough to sell at a good price, there was still the long, perilous journey back home through territory rife with robbers. Ohioans wanted a better transportation system—one that was reliable, available most of the year, and connected to eastern markets.[1]

Agitation for improved transportation in Ohio began in 1803, the year Ohio became a state. In that year a scheme was proposed to improve the channels of the Cuyahoga River, which flowed north into Lake Erie, and the Upper Muskingum (Tuscarawas River) and main Muskingum River, which flowed south to the Ohio River. The Cuyahoga and Tuscarawas Rivers were to be connected at their closest point by a seven-mile wagon road. The first state legislature authorized a private company to hold a lottery to raise the necessary $64,000 for the project. Unfortunately, there were not enough people in the state then with ready cash to raise such a stupendous sum. After a few years, with the work not even begun, the project was abandoned.

In 1807 Thomas Worthington, the U.S. senator from Ohio, introduced a bill directing the secretary of the treasury, Albert Gallatin, to investigate and report back to Congress on a plan for developing a system of federally sponsored canals and highways to link the "West" with the East. On April 4, 1808, Gallatin presented his now-famous "Report on Roads, Canals, Harbors, and Rivers." In it, he approved all the popular projects under consideration and suggested others that would have benefited nearly every state in the union. Gallatin believed that the whole scheme could be paid for in 10 years out of normal government revenue.

Conditions were changing, however, even while the various states lined up to get their share of the money. The U.S. Embargo Act, which had closed the nation's ports to foreign shipping in retaliation for having its ships stopped by foreign vessels at sea, was beginning to hurt U.S.

commerce. Congress didn't believe it would be prudent to undertake large projects and expenditures at such a time. Gallatin's recommendations were not followed. Political conditions soon escalated into the War of 1812 with Great Britain, and all the grandiose plans for internal improvement of the nation's transportation system were shelved. By the time the country and economy returned once more to some degree of normalcy, administrations (and attitudes) had changed in Washington—the federal government was no longer willing to finance and construct a network of canals and highways. Individual states were encouraged to handle their transportation needs on their own.

New York was one state in which citizens were determined to improve their transportation system—even if that meant financing a canal on their own. New Yorkers, however, were not against receiving outside help if it could be obtained. So in 1816 Thomas Worthington, who was then governor of Ohio, received a letter from the New York State Canal Commission requesting financial help to construct a canal from Albany to some point on Lake Erie. A committee appointed by the Ohio legislature studied the request and returned a favorable report. Four days later, however, the Ohio Senate struck out the portion of a resolution offering financial aid. Even so, a close relationship developed between New York canal commissioner DeWitt Clinton and Ohio governors Thomas Worthington (1814–18) and Ethan Allen Brown (1818–22).

Worthington and Brown marshaled their forces and agitated for a canal connecting Lake Erie to the Ohio River. Various committees were formed to study the project and several resolutions were proposed, but it wasn't until January 31, 1822, that the Ohio legislature passed an act authorizing surveys to be run over five specified routes.[2] The act of 1822 authorized the newly formed Ohio Canal Commission to hire an "expert engineer" to oversee the surveys. Unfortunately, in 1822 the state of Ohio could not boast of a single engineering school within its borders. (In fact, there was probably not one professional engineer living in Ohio at the time.) Fortunately, and due to the good offices of DeWitt Clinton, Ohio was able to employ one of New York State's top engineers, James Geddes, to oversee Ohio's canal surveys.

Geddes and one or more of Ohio's canal commissioners ran over 900 miles of surveys during the next nine months. However, at the end of 1822, Geddes was called back to New York without having examined all the possible routes specified in the act of 1822. The next year, the legislature passed a supplementary act to provide $4,000 in additional funds to complete the surveys, but Ohio was unable to obtain a senior engineer from New York to oversee the project. Each of Ohio's two active canal commissioners, Micajah T. Williams and Alfred E. Kelley, made trips to the Erie Canal during 1823 to gain firsthand knowledge about canal building.

That spring, the state of Ohio hired Seymour Skiff, an engineer from New York, to head the Ohio Engineering Corps. Unfortunately, the young man was in the field for only 14 days when he became infected with a disease (possibly malaria) that nearly every member of the surveying team contracted that year. Skiff was taken to Worthington to receive medical attention but died shortly thereafter. His death and the illness of crew members meant scant progress was made toward completing the surveys during the remainder of 1823. It took another season for the surveying to be completed and a final report to be made—a season in which the nucleus of an Ohio engineering staff was formed around another young engineer from the Erie Canal, William Price, and a young Ohioan, Samuel Forrer.

At the first Ohio Canal Commission meeting in 1822, the commissioners decided to run the proposed transportation system through as many established communities as possible so that more Ohioans could benefit from the system. With this in mind, the commissioners proposed a route that would start at Lake Erie, run up the Cuyahoga River Valley, and then, at the summit, travel to the Ohio River by one of two routes. The first route would lead east to the Ohio River through Columbiana County and the influential town of New Lisbon. The second would run southwesterly, crossing the Scioto Valley as far north of Columbus as possible and then along the valley of the Miami River until it reached the Ohio River at Cincinnati.

Once in the field, survey teams located a possible route for the canal from the Cuyahoga River summit to the Scioto Valley. However, the route crossed that valley some 11 miles *below* Columbus. From there, though they examined many routes, the surveyors were unable to find a sufficient supply of water to run a canal route to the valley of the Miami River or to run one from the summit of the Cuyahoga through New Lisbon.

A compromise had to be made. The Commissioners' Report of 1829 proposed what was considered to be a politically acceptable canal system from Lake Erie to the Ohio River. The state legislature passed a canal act in 1825 that, in effect, authorized two lake-to-river canals. The Ohio Canal would serve the eastern and central parts of the state.[3] It was what remained of the commissioners' diagonal route and would leave Lake Erie by way of the Cuyahoga or Black River Valley, run south via one of the branches of the Upper Muskingum (either Killbuck or Tuscarawas) to the main Muskingum River, then over the separating headlands to the Scioto Valley via the valleys of several smaller streams, or perhaps a tunnel through the dividing ridge, and then down the Scioto Valley to the Ohio River near Portsmouth. There would also be a sidecut canal up the Scioto Valley to Columbus, the state capital. A second canal would serve the relatively populous and politically powerful southwestern corner and eventually the whole western half of the state. It would follow the Miami River Valley north from the Ohio River at Cincinnati to or near Dayton. This second canal, the Miami Canal, was to be extended to Lake Erie, "at a later date."[4]

Less than five months later, on July 4, 1825, a celebrative ground breaking was held in a cleared spot within a heavily wooded area near the present town of Heath (southwest of Newark). A cheering throng had gathered to witness New York's Governor Clinton and Ohio's Governor Morrow turn the first spadefuls of earth, an act that officially began work on the Ohio Canal. Volunteers filled a wheelbarrow full of dirt, which they emptied at a future canal embankment. Thus the state of Ohio embarked on an ambitious program of artificial waterways that, together with privately financed projects, would total more than 1,000 miles and, as one prominent Ohio canal historian put it, would "bring the world to the wilderness."[5]

Planning the Route

The Canal Enabling Act of 1825 specified that the Ohio Canal should begin near the Licking Summit. However, the canal commissioners decided early on to construct and open the canal in segments from north to south, starting at Lake Erie, so that communications with the eastern markets could begin immediately upon the opening of that first section. The canal act had been vague in specifying the exact route the canal was to take from the lake to the forks of the Muskingum (the junction of the Walhonding and Tuscarawas Rivers) near present-day Coshocton. Therefore, the state canal commissioners had to locate the exact route of the canal between these two points before they could ready the sections for bidding.

The canal could have taken any of three routes between the forks of the Muskingum and Lake Erie. One of these was up the valleys of the Walhonding and Killbuck, across the watershed, and then down the valley of the Black to Lake Erie. The second was up the valley of the Tuscarawas, across the divide at the old Indian Portage, and then down the valley of the Cuyahoga to Lake Erie. The third possible route was up the valleys of the Walhonding and Killbuck, then across the Continental Divide, and down the valley of the Cuyahoga River to the lake. Each of the three possible routes had certain advantages, but it was water, or rather the availability of it, that dictated the final decision. Both routes involving the Killbuck would require extensive reservoir and feeder systems to provide sufficient water for the summit crossing. These would have been expensive to construct and maintain. Also, a break in a long feeder supplying a summit could dry up that level and shut the canal down during its busiest season.

Another point considered was that any feeder taken from the Cuyahoga River to supply a canal's summit level could seriously harm the many important water-powered industries then located along the river. Still, there were extensive swamps and several small natural lakes on the summit level between the Tuscarawas and Cuyahoga River Valleys. The canal engineers determined that the lakes in the area, plus portions of the swamp itself, could be easily and cheaply impounded and enlarged to feed sufficient water into the canal for the busiest seasons. Therefore, the Cuyahoga and Tuscarawas Valleys were chosen to carry the canal between Lake Erie and the forks of the Muskingum. Except for some minor details, the route was fixed.

These details, however, kept the canal commissioners and their engineers busy for quite some time. In holding to their objective of serving as many Ohioans as possible with the canal, the commissioners did not object to rerouting the line slightly to include a town that would otherwise be missed, as long as the change was technically feasible and did not materially increase the cost. To effect that change, the citizens of many bypassed towns were perfectly willing to make a substantial donation to the canal fund, which the commissioners gladly accepted.

When the residents of a tiny village at the junction of the Cuyahoga

River and Lake Erie contributed some $5,000 to the canal fund, the line of the canal was extended four or five miles down the eastern bank of the Cuyahoga to terminate at that village, Cleveland. The residents of Circleville pledged $3,500 to the canal fund if the commissioners would reroute the line through their southern Ohio town along the east side of the Scioto River, and the citizens and political leaders of Pike County and Chillicothe pressured the commissioners to route the canal along the west side of the Scioto through Chillicothe to the Ohio River. The commissioners yielded to the petitions from both areas. As a result, the canal passed through Circleville, then crossed the river on a great five-span aqueduct, and ran down the west bank of the Scioto through Chillicothe and Waverly, with the southern canal terminus on the opposite bank of the Scioto River from Portsmouth. The canal commissioners also cooperated with communities such as Zoar and Granville in making the planned feeders near those towns navigable so that extensions to each could be made by private groups.

Not every request for a route change was approved. It made good political sense to route the canal through New Philadelphia, the seat of government for Tuscarawas County. The commissioners and engineers expended a considerable amount of time and effort studying the problem of how best to connect New Philadelphia with the main canal, which until this point had been planned to run on the opposite, or right, bank of the Tuscarawas River through the rival community of Dover. The engineers finally decided there wasn't a safe, economical way to have the canal cross the Tuscarawas at this point. New Philadelphia was bypassed, but the commissioners promised to cooperate with any private company that would build a sidecut canal into the town.[6]

Engineering

The initial planning of the canal's route and the engineering were performed at the same time. The basic dimensions of any particular canal system were based largely on two criteria: the maximum amount of tonnage that the canal was expected to handle at peak season and the amount of water that could be brought to any portion of the line. Since each boat's passage through a lock sent a lock-full of water down the canal, lock dimensions needed to be kept as small as possible yet big enough to accommodate boats large enough to handle anticipated business. Similarly, the canal's channel had to be deep and wide enough to allow two boats to pass each other, yet the earthen sides of the embankments had to be sloped steeply enough (without causing excessive erosion) to economize on the amount of material the embankments required. The banks also had to be able to prevent water from filtering through them. The width of the bottom of the channel was generally twice the width of a boat, and the minimum depth was one foot greater than the submerged depth of a fully loaded boat.[7]

Considering the remote sites involved, the type of equipment available, and the relative lack of engineering data and mathematical tools, Ohio canal engineers of 1825 had many more serious impediments than did railroad engineers a half century later or the highway engineers of today. Fortunately for the engineers designing the Ohio & Erie Canal, many of the problems they would encounter had already been resolved by designers of New York's Erie Canal some eight years earlier. Canvass White, one of New York's most promising young engineers, traveled to England in 1817 to observe and record details on the design and operation of British canals. White returned the next year with a set of new surveying instruments and a vast quantity of carefully made drawings describing various canal structures and engineering features.[8]

The greatest deviation the Erie engineers made from the British designs was in the size of the locks and channel. The majority of the English canals used locks that were 60 feet long by 8 to 12 feet wide. The New Yorkers established lock chamber dimensions of 90 feet by 15 feet. This allowed boats 85 feet by 14 feet to navigate the Erie Canal carrying cargoes of approximately 50 tons. The great Erie Canal opened for navigation in sections from 1819 through 1825. Everywhere that the water flowed and boats floated, there was success and money.[9]

With much of its engineering corps taken from New York plans and with that magnificent example literally staring them in the face across Lake Erie, Ohio adopted the engineering of the Erie Canal nearly whole cloth, with only a few differences. Ohio engineers "cheated" a bit by making the channel's bottom width only 26 feet. The slope of the interior embankment walls was thus shallower than that of the Erie and less susceptible to erosion.

When the Ohio Canal was first proposed, there was serious doubt whether this young state could afford to construct its canals using finished stone for the locks and culverts. It was thought that these structures would first have to be constructed using a combination of rough stone and wood and later be rebuilt more permanently after canal traffic brought in sufficient funds. However, an initial bond issue in 1825 sold well in the eastern U.S. and British money markets, with the promise that future issues would sell equally well. Therefore, the canal commissioners decided to build the Ohio Canal with first-class materials.

There was a compromise made in the design of aqueducts, however. Instead of all the components—arches, supports, and waterways—being built of stone masonry, aqueducts on the Ohio Canal became wooden troughs, supported by masonry piers and abutments and barely wide enough for a single boat to traverse. Ohio's engineers also made what they considered improvements in their mixing of hydraulic lime (cement that would harden under water), a method for automatically passing water from one level to another around locks through "regulating channels," and the newer design for embankments.

The first bonds released for financing canal construction sold well enough, but to ensure a good sale for succeeding bond issues, the canal commissioners decided to concentrate the first phase of construction on the section of canal adjacent to Lake Erie. They wanted to get at least a portion of the canal open and carrying traffic as early as possible. In that way, Ohio produce would flow out of the canal, across the lake to Buffalo, and then down the Erie Canal to eastern markets. This would be excellent publicity to enhance the sale of future bond issues. It would also earn a modicum of money through tolls for the fledgling system.[10]

PREPARING FOR CONSTRUCTION

The actual construction of the canal was performed entirely by private contractors. However, the final surveys, the measuring of the types of work and materials required, the laying out of the canal line, and the general superintendence were all in the hands of state-employed engineers and assistants, under the direction of the acting canal commissioners.

A canal was required to run on a nearly level plane. Earth from cuttings was transported to areas that needed to be built up. Ideally, the amount of earth from cuttings would equal the amount needed to build up low areas. But in reality there was always a bit more cutting or fill required than the immediate terrain provided. The straighter canals were more expensive because they required extra fill or cutting. An economically constructed canal was crooked, following the contour of the land. The actual line a canal took was an engineer's compromise of a direct route and the economics of construction.

As soon as the decision was made to concentrate forces on the northernmost section of the canal, resident engineer William H. Price began a careful, final location of the line. Lock sites were determined relatively early in the route location process. When levels taken along the line indicated that the terrain had dropped approximately six feet, engineers began looking for the proper location and soil conditions for a lock. When they found such a spot, they drove a sturdy wooden stake into the earth at the head of the lock site. The top of the stake would represent the level of the surface of the towpath, the surface of the water, or the bottom of the channel. To make information readily available to all concerned, the engineers carved data into prominent trees on each level, indicating the elevations of the bottom of the canal, the surface of the water, and the surface of the towpath. The marks were called bench levels, and their locations, the species of trees they were cut in, and other relevant information were recorded in the engineer's field notes.

Once the locks were located, the engineering staff drove a series of stakes into the earth to indicate the river side (towpath) of the canal's bottom and another set of stakes 26 feet away to indicate the opposite side (berm bank) of the bottom. When the line of canal was straight, the stakes were offset from each other by about ten paces. When the line was curved, the stakes were set closer together.[11]

For the most part, the route of the Ohio Canal ran through the lowlands of the various river valleys from Lake Erie to the Ohio River. These lowlands were seldom settled or farmed during the early nineteenth century. There were thick stands of gigantic trees, all tied together with tangles of wild grapevines and impenetrable underbrush. Flood waters would stay in these lands nearly all year in the form of marshes and swamps. The periodic flooding deposited great amounts of fertile soil that only aided the heavy undergrowth. These lowlands were veritable pest houses, breeding all manner of disease and pestilence.[12] This made it relatively easy to obtain right-of-way for the route at little or no cost, but it made a canal worker's plight difficult, often wet, and sometimes fatal.

Price's staff next divided the stretch of canal into sections. Normally, each section contained 30 to 40 chains, about a half mile of channel, or one heavy bit of construction, such as a lock, culvert, or river dam. Formal drawings for each section were prepared, containing a plan and elevation view. The staff prepared an estimate for each type of work required in the section and the estimated costs for each. Then, as they were ready, stretches of canal sections were advertised for bids in local and eastern papers and in publicly displayed handbills. An engineering office was set up in the vicinity, where private contractors could obtain bid packages, examine the line, and submit their bids. After a deadline had passed, the bids were opened and the contracts awarded.[13]

Between June 10 and July 29, 1825, contracts were let on canal sections from the Summit Pond (present-day Summit Lake in Akron) for a little over 33 miles to a point near the village of Newburgh, some seven miles south of Lake Erie. A lively debate followed on whether to end the canal there, cross to the west bank of the river, and run down to the lake (a more feasible engineering solution) or to continue down the east bank of the river and terminate in the rival village of Cleveland. Finally, in February 1826, after the residents of Cleveland donated $5,000 to the canal fund, the decision was made to extend the canal down the east bank of the river to that village. The contracts for the extension were let in February 1826, including two more locks. The contracts for the final two locks (for a total of 44 in this stretch) connecting the canal with the Cuyahoga River and Lake Erie were let in March 1827.[14]

Contracts south of the Summit Pond were let in two groups during 1826. By year's end, the canal was under contract as far south as two miles below Blakes Mills (present-day south New Philadelphia) in Tuscarawas County, 95 miles from the northern terminus. Nearly 2,000 men and 3,000 teams of horses and oxen were working on the canal between Cleveland and Kendall (Massillon) in Stark County.

During 1825 and 1826, an additional 1,200 men and a large number of oxen were also at work on a three-mile Deep Cut, some seven miles below the Licking Summit to assure that hard-to-get items would be available in time for the rest of the canal. Contracts continued to be let in sections, north to south from the Portage Summit and south to north from the Licking Summit, then from the Deep Cut, south to Portsmouth as quickly as the engineers could survey, stake out the line, and prepare drawings.[15]

The northern section of the canal, as it contained more of the tougher and costlier sections, attracted more contractors from the Erie Canal. Over 50 percent of the contracts let between Summit Pond and Lake Erie were from the state of New York. Since most of these contractors brought their crews with them, many workmen on this stretch of the canal were from Ireland via the Erie Canal. The majority of the men receiving contracts for sections south of Kendall, however, were Ohioans. Of the workers on those canal sections on and north of the Licking Summit, one historian commented on the lack of foreigners in the mix and was pleased that "nearly all are native-born Americans." When contracts were first let on the Licking Summit, early in the construction phase, men came to work on the canal from as far away as Fairfield, Hocking, Gallia, and Meigs Counties, as well as from all over the country. Ohio farmers and their sons wanted to earn the cash wages, as it was a scarce commodity on the frontier. For some things, such as taxes, cash was the only form of payment accepted.[16]

By the time canal construction had progressed south to the Scioto Valley, Irish and German workers had joined the effort and were mentioned often in reports. Each contract on the first two sections let received an average of three or more bids. Those let in 1826 received more than 50 bids for each contract offered. As a result, the majority of the contracts were let at prices well below estimate. This pleased the engineers, of course. Unfortunately, some contractors' bids were so low that they were forced to abandon their jobs. A grievous number absconded without paying their workers. This forced the state to rebid those contracts at higher prices and delayed completion at many points along the line.[17]

CONSTRUCTION

Canal digging was not a pleasant occupation even at the best of times. The canal diggers often had to work all day in water, and malarial diseases were common among the workers. C. C. Morgan, a popular steamship captain and businessman in the Dresden-Zanesville river trade during the latter part of the nineteenth century, got his start as a 15-year-old canal digger on the Ohio Canal near Newark in 1826. In a letter to a friend, he wrote, "I am cold, wet and sleepy. My head aches so that I am almost insensible to everything around me."[18]

The construction season began as soon as the earth thawed in the spring. The crew worked hard through the spring and into summer until mid-July, when malaria and ague forced the crew to temporarily suspend their work. After the first frost, work began again and was carried on until heavy snows and cold once again shut things down.

Workers were at first paid $8 a month for 26 sunrise-to-sunset days. Crew members worked hard and were well fed and lodged, usually in temporary shanties set up along the line. During the construction of the Ohio Canal, wages fluctuated by area and demand, finally rising in 1831 to about $15 a month.[19] The types of work described in the majority of contracts included lock and culvert construction, excavation and embankment, grubbing and clearing, mucking and ditching, and puddling and protection.

Often, masonry structures, such as locks, culverts, and aqueduct supports, were begun before the easier jobs of earth excavation and embankment. Whenever possible, the masonry structures were constructed on and tied into a solid rock foundation. When this was impossible, pilings were driven into the earth, and a sturdy foundation of timber and puddle was constructed on them. All lift locks on the Ohio Canal were of interlocked double-wall stone masonry with the inside chamber of finished dressed stone. Several of the guard locks were of "alligator" construction—stone gate supports with earthen and riprap centers. The construction of the locks was labor intensive, from the digging of the deep lock pits to the lifting and positioning of the great lock stones (with the help of animal power), which were swung into place with long, towering pole cranes.[20]

All contractors doing dry work, where the channel and embankments would be above the natural surface of the earth, were required to grub the entire area. Also, they had to clear all growth more than a foot high for 20 feet on either side of this line so there was no danger of anything falling across the channel later and obstructing navigation. Large trees were felled with axes, which were cheaper than saws. When possible, tree removal took place in winter, when axes met less resistance from sap flow and when snow and less foliage eased log removal. Similarly, stumps were generally pulled in early spring, when the soil was most sodden and undergrowth was least present. A cutting plow was used to break up the roots for grubbing, and a harrow was sometimes employed to gather them. Oxen were usually the motive power of choice as they could pull more than horses, were less prone to disease, and were more plentiful on farms in Ohio during the 1820s.[21]

It doesn't appear as if stump-pulling machinery or other mechanical gadgets mentioned in stories of constructing the Erie Canal made it across Lake Erie to Ohio. Norman Newell Hill, in his *History of Licking County* (1881), relates the tale of one of the more important landowners of the county taking several sections of the canal line at the southern end of the summit. He at once obtained "machinery" to remove a large stand of elm trees. After several failed attempts to make the machinery work, he had to resort to old and tested tree-removal methods, namely axes and shovels wielded by many men. As a result, the contractor lost a considerable sum of money because the job took longer and required more men than anticipated.

When the channel and embankments were to be constructed below the natural surface of the earth, it was necessary to clear out the muck and dig ditches along the line. These ditches were filled with earth to provide a solid base for the embankments. Workers on swampy sections had the hardest and most disease-ridden job of all and perhaps coined the phrase "mucking about." Oddly enough, the line of the canal on both summits ran through extensive swamps.[22]

There was a great deal of difficulty digging the channel through the Portage Summit swamp. The level of the Summit Pond was to be dropped some nine feet to keep the summit as low as possible. Those sections immediately below the pond, however, couldn't be let for contract until other contractors, using a kiln in the line of canal to burn hydraulic lime, had completed their operation. Then, when the pond finally was lowered, a temporary dam gave way prematurely, causing much flooding and damage.[23]

The Deep Cut along the swamp on the Licking Summit required the removal of vast quantities of a tough, blue clay. Several contractors went broke on the job. Eventually, a system of oxen-powered tramways was set up, but it still took nearly four years before the Deep Cut on the Licking Summit was finished.[24]

Recorded narratives of Ohio's canal workers often relate, "We did it all with draft animals and wheelbarrows." Plows pulled by horses or oxen loosened the earth. A long string of men pushing wheelbarrows that trundled between other workers who shoveled the loose earth into the barrows and the dumping points where an embankment was being constructed. One historian commented, "It was a sight to see fifty of these barrow-men in a string wheeling out their heavy loads, following a leader who always made it warm for them." Barrow men often wore iron band "creepers" on their feet to keep from slipping off the planking back into the ditch.[25]

Constructing a canal often required more than just digging or preparing a ditch. If the resident engineer felt a section was suspect or if trials showed a section wouldn't hold water, then the bottom and parts of the banks were lined with clay puddle. Also, all outside embankments that were subject to erosion were protected with a covering of loose stone, pavement, or riprap.[26]

☼ 2 ☼
Early Operation

OPENING

Loans to build the initial stages of the Ohio & Erie Canal had been obtained relatively easily in New York in 1825. A national economic depression the following year, however, slowed Ohio Canal bond sales. Also, a few absconding canal contractors and the inevitable disease among workmen had slowed work on the project. By early 1827, construction on the Ohio Canal had been under way for almost two years and no portion had yet been completed. Those responsible for selling Ohio's future canal bonds wanted something to show prospective investors. They wanted to showcase canal boats traversing at least a portion of the Ohio Canal, transporting the riches of the state's interior to the newly improved lake port of Cleveland. The canal commissioners therefore decided to officially open the canal from the Portage Summit to Cleveland, some 37 miles to the north, on the nation's birthday, July 4, 1827, even though several of the canal's major structures were as yet unfinished.[1]

Grandiose plans were made for the great day. The Cleveland firm of Merwin and Giddings had a boat built prior to the opening of the canal at the present-day town of Peninsula and christened it the *Pioneer*. That same firm also purchased a boat from the Erie Canal and had it transported to Cleveland where it was christened the *Allen Trimble*. The Wheeler brothers of Portage County built a boat below the first lock to the north of the Portage Summit, launched it on June 27, 1827, and christened it the *State of Ohio*.

Many boats were being constructed along the line of the canal, freight was piling up, and transportation lines were being developed and expanded to handle the tonnage. It was the *State of Ohio* that left the basin below Lock 1 on July 3, 1827, met the *Pioneer* that night in Boston, and then joined the *Allen Trimble* some six miles north of Cleveland after the latter craft had been dragged from the Cuyahoga River and launched into the canal. These three boats composed the inaugural flotilla on the Ohio Canal.[2]

Vast throngs of people lined the banks of the canal for much of the last six miles of that journey. But it was at the temporary termination below the bluffs that held Cleveland's main buildings where the real celebrating began. (The vast terminal basin and outlet locks into the river weren't as yet completed.) It ended many hours later and a few blocks east and north, at Belden's Tavern and the Franklin House, where numerous toasts were made to the wonderful accomplishment for which everyone present felt a personal satisfaction.[3]

However, the most important event of that day was the arrival of the *Enterprise,* a freight boat commanded by Captain Guy. The boat docked in Cleveland shortly after the celebrating throng had departed. Loaded with flour and whiskey from Akron, the *Enterprise* inaugurated commercial traffic on the Ohio Canal.

Opening day and "first boat" celebrations were repeated over the next five years as completed sections of the canal were opened to traffic. The celebration at Massillon in Stark County on August 27, 1828, was a big one. The *Allen Trimble* and the *State of Ohio*, loaded with visiting dignitaries, were the focal point.

The waters of the Ohio Canal reached Dover in Tuscarawas County on October 29, 1829. Christian Deardorf, the town's founder and contractor of a section of the work nearby, had built a "large and commodious boat" on the banks of the dry ditch and christened it the *Union*. It was launched sideways into the canal as soon as water levels were sufficient. Reporters exclaimed that "most of the county's residents turned out to line the banks" as the *Union* left its home port for the north and Cleveland.[4]

Flooding on the Walhonding in late 1829 so damaged the aqueduct and feeder that the canal's completion through to Newark was delayed. Finally, on July 10, 1830, the section of canal from the Deep Cut in Licking County to Dover was opened. The first boat through Nashport, Muskingum County, was the *Reindeer*, a pleasure boat built in Newark and taken to Coshocton to sell. The first commercial craft through the canal in Muskingum County from the north was the *Union* out of Dover.

Caldersburg (the present Roscoe Village portion of Coshocton) celebrated the opening of the Ohio Canal on August 21, 1830. The *Monticello*, unable to cross the Walhonding River into town due to continuing problems with the aqueduct and feeder, "remained several days attracting wonder-struck visitors from all this [Coshocton] County and even adjoining counties."[5]

Twenty miles of canal from the beginning of the Deep Cut on the Licking Summit through Newark to the "Narrows of the Licking" were filled with water on May 26, 1829, but sections to the north were not finished for more than a year and those to the south for more than two years. Canal communication with the north was completed in July 1830 but was sporadic for some time due to problems with the Walhonding Aqueduct. Newark remained the lower end of navigation on the Ohio Canal for more than a year, mainly due to delays in completing the Deep Cut on the Licking Summit. Then, on September 19, 1831, water was let into the canal through Circleville. The two large basins in town were filled in 45 minutes. Amid the discharge of artillery and the shouts of the vast crowd gathered to witness the occasion, the guard gate was opened and the water admitted to the aqueduct across the Scioto. The *Governor Brown* was launched in Circleville on September 20, and the next day, filled with passengers, it made a trial run to Scioto Bluffs. On September 27 two boats came down from the Licking Summit, and the next day 12 visiting craft arrived from the north to take part in the local rejoicing.[6]

The sidecut to Columbus was opened just a few days earlier on September 23, 1831. The *Governor Brown*, filled with "the most respectable citizens of Pickaway County," arrived from Circleville and was celebrated by the firing of a cannon. Two days later, the *Cincinnati, Red Rover,* and *Lady Jane* began regular freight service to Columbus. Until the main canal was opened south to the Ohio River, all goods for the west went by canal to Columbus, then by wagon to Dayton, and finally by the Miami Canal to Cincinnati and the Ohio River.[7]

Chillicothe, Ohio's capital for all but two years between 1803 and 1818, was still a hotbed of political agitation in the 1820s. When the canal com-

missioners planned to route the Ohio Canal down the opposite bank of
the Scioto—bypassing Chillicothe—the outcry was enough to convince
the commissioners to rethink their plans. The canal was then relocated to
the west bank of the Scioto. This meant its southern terminus would be on
the opposite river bank from the town of Portsmouth in an area subject to
frequent flooding, but Chillicothe got the canal. Ceremonies to welcome
the opening of navigation to Chillicothe were held on October 22, 1831.
Reportedly, all previous opening celebrations paled in comparison.[8]

The 50 miles of canal between Chillicothe and the Ohio River at
Portsmouth proved to be one of the more difficult segments to complete.
Heavy flooding in February 1832 destroyed the partially completed line.
Much of the channel and many structures sustained heavy damage. The
spread of cholera to the Scioto Valley in July 1832 killed many of the canal
workers and drove the rest from their jobs.[9]

It was announced that water would be let into the canal above Waverly,
Ohio, on September 6, 1832. Almost the entire population of the surrounding country came to town to line the canal banks and wait for the water.
The gravelly, porous nature of the canal's new bed made the water's progress
slow, and it wasn't until around noon that it finally arrived. Shortly afterward, a small, crudely built boat arrived from Chillicothe with a number of
local citizens on board. Nobody remembered its name, but the residents did
recall that it had the unseaworthy tendency to sink each night and require
pumping out each morning.

The first official boat to arrive in Waverly was the *Governor Worthington,* another small boat (with only 25 tons capacity) from Chillicothe. A
small brass cannon mounted at the bow of the *Worthington* boomed again
and again as the crowd gathered around, "cheering like crazy people."[10]
Governor McArthur addressed the Whigs, and local politician Robert
Lucas, who succeeded McArthur as governor the next year, addressed the
Democrats. Later, Waverly's own James Emmitt opened his purse strings
and fed everyone, Whigs and Democrats alike, who appeared that day to
see the water arrive.[11]

Later, according to local legend, Emmitt grew "hilariously happy,"
opened his purse strings again, and purchased the *Governor Worthington*
on the spot for $600.[12] That same day he loaded his craft with Waverly
citizens and pointed the boat southward. He planned to pilot the first

boat to reach Portsmouth. Local legend states that at times Emmitt's boat ran ahead of the water. Finally, two miles short of Portsmouth, the *Worthington* so outdistanced the water that it couldn't catch up and the craft grounded.

A gala event in Portsmouth to celebrate the completion of the canal was scheduled for October 15, 1832. Massive flooding of the Ohio River and a recurrence of cholera in the region, however, forced a postponement. On December 1, 1832, rather quietly and with a lot less fanfare than had been anticipated, the Ohio Canal was completed from Cleveland to Portsmouth.[13]

EARLY OPERATION, 1827–1839

The citizens along the Ohio Canal literally leaped into action long before the canal was completed through to the Ohio River. A few boatyards had been set up at various points between Akron and Cleveland, and a number of craft were available as soon as the canal opened between those two points. Transportation lines were set up, each consisting of a number of suitable craft, warehousing facilities, and forwarding and receiving houses. In many cases connections extended from the New York canal all along the Ohio.[14]

Available sources indicate that in October 1831, when the canal had just been opened to Circleville and Columbus, there were approximately 45 boats operating. This number rapidly increased when the full canal opened the next year. It also appears that independent boatmen were not all that common, at least in the very early days of canal operation. Nearly every craft was affiliated with a line, mill, or other business. This affiliation ranged from the New Philadelphia Mills (a one-boat operation) to the Ohio, Troy, and Erie line that controlled 22 boats in the late 1830s. Even the separatist society at Zoar owned four canal boats in the 1840s.[15]

The standard lock size on the Ohio Canal was 15 feet by 90 feet. The size of the boats was therefore limited to a maximum of 14½ feet by 85 feet. At first, the boats were built somewhat smaller than the maximum allowable dimensions, with rather sharp prows and slim lines. This made towing easier and the boats quicker. A boat's maximum cargo capacity was around 30 to 50 tons.

Initially, canal boats were operated day and night between Cleveland and points south as the canal was extended. Each trip to Akron took between 15 and 20 hours. Later trips to Portsmouth took an average of 7 to 9 days. The majority of these early craft were set up to carry both passengers and freight. Those that carried passengers were often called "packets," though a swift, express packet line between Cleveland and Portsmouth wasn't available until the beginning of the 1837 boating season. Two-thirds of the craft operated by the five major freight and passenger lines in 1835 were set up to carry both freight and passengers; only one-third of the boats hauled exclusively freight. Many of these line boat passengers were immigrants coming to the "new west" from Europe and the eastern United States.

Very little of the freight carried in that era was in bulk form. Nearly everything was packed in barrels, baskets, or bales. Therefore, most boats were completely enclosed. They had a long cabin, or house, built from bow to stern that could be divided into several compartments for carrying both freight and passengers. These boats, called two-deckers, had a deck on top of the cabin and the deck of the interior hold. So identified was this type of craft with the formal freight and passenger lines that long after those lines had ceased operation, this type of Ohio Canal boat was referred to as a "line boat." Boating was initially considered an elite trade. Many young men in Ohio from the early 1830s into the mid-1840s could think of no loftier goal than that of being the captain of a line boat. They dressed as dandies and were highly respected and envied by nearly everyone they met.[16]

Toll offices were set up at intervals along the canal to regulate commerce. In theory, all freight and passengers carried on the Ohio Canal were carefully logged. Freight was regulated by bills of lading that were checked at each toll office. No freight was to be unloaded without the proper signed certificate, and no boat was allowed to travel the canal without proper documentation. Fines were imposed for all violations. In practice, however, many boatmen liked to see how much they could get away with. At least one boatman operated only between the toll stations of Cleveland and Akron, thus avoiding paying a toll at either location. At toll stations that depended on portable scales, "move and hide the cargo" became a popular game among boatmen.

Regulations were also set up for the proper way to pass another boat on the canal, for determining which boat had the right-of-way, and for precedence at locks. When the rules didn't work, fistfights often erupted.

Seven crewmen were required to operate an early freight boat and usually nine to operate a packet. Often a boat would carry one or more crewmen whose main duty was to enforce the rights of their boat if the rules and regulations didn't work.[17] The state of Ohio did not employ formal lock tenders during the early canal days. A crewman simply ran ahead and ensured that the lock was aligned correctly and belonged to them. The "discussion" of who owned a lock was also often settled with fisticuffs.[18]

The economic climate in Ohio during the late 1820s and early 1830s was good, and the canals were free from most serious competition. Still, the owners of a number of canal lines weren't making as much money as they felt they could or should. In an effort to minimize expenses, four of the major transportation lines formed a loose consortium in January 1835. One of the big expenses was in the cost of towing. In the early days of operation on the Ohio Canal, towing animals were stationed at way stations along the canal at intervals of 12 to 15 miles. Many boat lines tried to economize by increasing the distance between way stations. Some boatmen worked their animals as much as 48 hours a stretch. This had a disastrous outcome on the health of the animals, and the cost of towing was still around 26½ cents a mile. The Canal Line Consortium pooled their animals in an attempt to economize on towing expenses. The experiment failed to result in any significant savings, however. Finally, one unsung hero devised a plan to carry a spare team onboard the boat. This reduced a boat's cargo capacity somewhat, but it reduced towing expenses by two-thirds, to about 7 cents per mile. Two additional boat lines joined the consortium in 1836, and the total number of boats under their control peaked at 66. The fleet of this consortium then accounted for more than half of all freight and passenger movement on the canal.[19]

The economy of the nation and the state boomed into the beginning of 1837. By the next year, an estimated 340 boats were operating on the Ohio Canal alone. Many of the villages that sprung up along the Ohio Canal found their businesses and populations rapidly expanding. It was a time of unbridled enthusiasm and optimism. In March 1837, the Ohio Canal Packet Boat Company was organized as a stock company in Cleveland with a capital of $50,000 to provide the first true express-packet service on the Ohio Canal. Practice runs had been made the previous year between Cleveland and Hebron using sharper-prowed, easier-to-tow craft constructed for the speedy passenger trade. Thus, a second type of craft became visible on the Ohio Canal: the passenger packet.[20]

A system of way stations was set up the entire length of the canal, and a fleet of eight express passenger packets was acquired. This line advertised through passage from Cleveland to Portsmouth in a mere 80 hours. During 1838 and 1839, the state built small lock tenders' sheds at nearly all the lift locks on the Ohio Canal. For the next 20 years or so, lock tenders were stationed at nearly every one of the more than 150 lift locks on the Ohio Canal.[21]

Prosperity was rampant everywhere along the state canal system during the early and mid-1830s. Agitation from Ohio citizens for additional transportation lines grew even more intense after the Ohio Canal was completed in late 1832. It led to the formation of private companies that planned to build canals, turnpikes, and even that new mode of transportation, railways. Ohio's private sector was still short of investment funds, however, so these companies naturally turned to the state for financial assistance. The legislature's policy for a number of years was merely to grant a special charter to these fledgling transportation companies without offering any direct financial aid. Many of these charters were granted, some of which had no real chance of success. In fact, there were so many requests for charters that the state government was nearly unable to function properly, and those Ohio communities not on a canal route lobbied their representatives to obtain expansion of the existing canal system. Legislation in 1836 and 1837 remedied the situation. Even though enormous sums of money were still owed on the original system, the legislature gave in to pressure from the have-nots and authorized a vast, expensive program of canal expansion.[22]

Though the main Ohio Canal was now completed, three items of the expansion—the Muskingum River Improvement, the Walhonding Canal, and the Hocking Canal—were to be traffic feeders to the main canal. In addition, tolls from the Ohio Canal were used as much as possible to pay off the loans, and now the expansion program increased that requirement even more.

Then, on March 24, 1837, the state legislature passed the controversial Loan Law, which authorized the state to offer a "loan of credit" for up to one-third of the estimated cost of the project or up to 50 percent of the purchase price of stock of any private canal, turnpike, or rail company when half of the offered stock had been sold. Detractors called it the "plunder law." The Board of Public Works had to approve any projects in which the state was to purchase stock, but the Loan Law added millions to the state debt and accelerated the building of railroads throughout Ohio.[23]

In May 1837, due in large part to the unbridled era of economic expansion and frivolous speculation, the country's economy collapsed, creating a severe and long-lived panic. Many businesses throughout the country failed. In May, nearly every bank in the country closed and nearly half failed to reopen. Many of these banks and businesses (including the Ohio Packet Boat Company) had issued their own script, and most of it became worthless. People lost faith in paper monies, and most transactions throughout Ohio took place by the barter system. This general financial collapse lasted well into the next decade.[24]

Receipts on the Ohio Canal, however, continued to grow through 1840. Canal receipts increased, despite the devastating economic conditions, because the Ohio Canal was the only means of transportation into and out of the interior of the state until about 1840. There was also a great deal of through traffic from Lake Erie to the river system at Portsmouth, traffic the canal commissioners had counted on when initiating the state's canal system. The canal commissioners and eastern backers hoped the system would break Ohioans of their dependency on southern markets and tie the state to eastern markets and the Union. In 1834, the canal commissioners reported that there had been a great increase in the amount of through traffic on the Ohio Canal, "particularly the transportation of merchandise from the Lake to the Ohio River, on its way from eastern cities to the southwestern states."[25]

COMPETITION AND SECONDARY OPERATION, 1840–1856

Around 1840, the Ohio Canal experienced its first serious competition from other modes of long-distance transportation. First, the National Road, bisecting the Ohio Canal at Heath, just south of Newark, was becoming a more dependable east-west thoroughfare. Second, a great reduction in the cost of river transportation between New Orleans and the eastern markets put an effective stop to through traffic in both directions between Lake Erie and the Ohio River. In addition, the decision to route the Ohio Canal through as many towns as possible had proven in the long run to

be a mistake. The route from the lake to the river was longer than necessary, handicapping the canal's ability to compete with more direct routes.
Further, the water supply on the Licking Summit, near Newark, had never
been satisfactory. Even the construction of an additional reservoir in the
late 1830s did not solve the problem during dry periods.[26]

By the early 1840s, the traffic pattern on the canal had permanently
changed. For all practical purposes, goods at or south of Newark were
transported south on the canal to the river, and goods north of Newark
were transported to the lake.[27] The Pennsylvania & Ohio Canal, from the
Ohio Canal at Akron to the Pennsylvania Canal system at Mahoningtown,
near New Castle, opened as a through route between the two canal systems
in 1840. This route actually strengthened traffic on the northern section of
the Ohio Canal but reduced traffic in its southern section by adding the
Pittsburgh port (a Cleveland competitor) on the Ohio & Erie. In 1843, the
Muskingum Improvement opened and provided an additional, shorter
route between central Ohio and the river.[28]

Outside competition plus repercussions of the economic panics (which
eased slightly in 1840 but hit hard again in 1842) made a tremendous
impact on operations on the Ohio Canal. During the first three weeks of
April 1837, 250 businesses failed in New York alone. Some of these were
connected with canal lines in Ohio. Entire freight and passenger lines
were for sale at "good prices." The Ohio Canal Packet Boat Company
disappeared after 1839. Other through lines took its place for a few more
years, possibly using the same way stations and hiring some of the same
owners. The year 1842 was the last year that through passenger packets
operated between Cleveland and Portsmouth.

The poor economy forced changes. Several passenger lines cooperated
with each other—one line sent boats from Cleveland to a midpoint on
the canal and the other line sent connecting boats up from Portsmouth.[29]
Those freight and passenger lines that remained made additional changes.
New boats were constructed in the mid-1840s. Their overall dimensions
increased to the maximum and although they were slower, harder to tow,
and required a cleared canal channel to operate in, their capacities increased to 60 and 70 tons. A change of animals was carried onboard. Even
some of the express packets carried their spare teams "amid-ships."[30]

Since the canal began to depend more and more on traffic generated
from the interior of the state, harvest failures and declines in particular

commodity production had great effects on canal revenues. Wheat shipments fluctuated greatly during the 1840s, and corn, feathers, and pork fell off drastically. Fortunately, numerous drift and shaft mines were opened in Stark and Tuscarawas Counties in the late 1840s, and mineral coal became an important cargo to Lake Erie. Canal boats were altered or constructed with two open holds (one on either side of the spare team's stable), and the three-cabin freighter began appearing on the Ohio Canal with more and more frequency.[31]

After 1843, the country's economy steadily recovered. By 1847, total receipts of the Ohio Canal finally exceeded those generated in 1840. The year 1847 was the high point in revenue generation on the Ohio Canal, and only once in the 1840s was annual revenue below $300,000. That was in 1845, when receipts fell to a little over $260,000.[32] The Miami & Erie Canal, which opened in 1843 with a shorter route between the river and lake, generated much higher revenues than the Ohio Canal after 1845. Boaters and shippers on the Ohio Canal were back to enjoying good, if not great, profits through the end of the decade. However, after the mid-1840s, canal building in Ohio was over. The expansion of 1836–37 had placed a tremendous burden on the state's finances, and at least one of the expansion canal lines (the Walhonding Canal at Roscoe) was never completed as planned. The Loan Law was repealed in 1840, but its use had already increased the state debt considerably. By 1844, Ohio's debt, largely due to canal construction, stood at $19.28 million. Yet Ohio did not repudiate its debt as some other "western" states had.[33]

Due to the poor quality of building stone, a number of structures throughout the line required substantial maintenance, and a number of locks in the Newark area had to be rebuilt in the mid-1840s. It didn't help matters either that the Board of Public Works had to seek special legislation for anything more than general maintenance, such as flood repair and lock rebuilding, which slowed general upkeep of the canal system. Still, the general maintenance on the Ohio & Erie was good throughout the 1840s.[34]

After 1846, the economy had improved, so the state began levying taxes to pay off its debt. But the taxes fell on a generation that had not known the all-encompassing need for the canals as their fathers had. All they knew was that they were paying off a tremendous debt for a transportation system that, though it still appeared to be prospering, was soon to be outmoded and relegated to the past. Still, in spite of the grumblings from some areas of the state and, more ominously, from their legislative representatives, life on the Ohio Canal was prosperous through the end of the decade.[35]

The decade of the 1850s saw dramatic changes in canal tonnage, types of cargo carried, and finally, in operation. There had been interest in railroads in the state as early as 1826, but that technology hadn't been ready. Then, the economic panics of the late 1830s and early 1840s further delayed railroad development. With the improvement of the economy in the late 1840s, many of the old railroad plans were dusted off. The state legislature approved funds, and the rush to build railroads was on.

Beginning in the early 1850s, railroad competition hit the canals hard and often. The Sandusky, Mansfield & Newark Railroad began through operation from Newark, a vital shipping point on the Ohio Canal, to Lake Erie at Sandusky in 1851. Officials of the railroad quickly offered faster and cheaper service to a lake port than did the canal, resulting in grain shipments north on the canal from Newark falling to less than half of what they had been before 1851.[36]

Total tonnage shipped on the Ohio Canal actually increased during the early 1850s, with coal more than making up the loss in grain shipments. This drastic shift in cargo content had a long-range effect on the Ohio & Erie Canal. Coal was a relatively short-haul commodity, from the coalfields along the Hocking Branch Canal or from the mines of Tuscarawas and Stark Counties along the northern reaches of the Ohio Canal to Lake Erie or local industries situated on the canal. Forwarders, warehousemen, and long-haul freight lines felt the pinch. Many of them closed. More and more three-cabin freighters were seen on the canal now, many of which were captained by independent haulers. The last boat-building boom on the Ohio Canal was seen in the early 1850s. In fact, the total number of boats operating on the Ohio Canal in 1856 approached or possibly exceeded the number operating in those halcyon days of 1838.[37]

Tolls on coal, however, were low and, since hauls were relatively short, overall receipts on the Ohio & Erie Canal fell. The Toledo & Western Railroad opened along the route of the Miami & Erie Canal, diverting more than half of the wheat, corn, and oats carried to Toledo. In 1856, incoming receipts for all of Ohio's canals fell below maintenance expenditures for the first time, though receipts on the Ohio Canal did not fall below expenditures until 1858. The Cleveland & Mahoning Railroad gained control of the Pennsylvania & Ohio Canal in 1858. Tolls on that canal were raised so high as to divert all business to the railroad. Business that had previously been funneled into the Ohio Canal at Akron was lost. The Tuscarawas branch of the Cleveland & Pittsburgh Railroad came into direct competition with the Ohio & Erie Canal between Akron and Canal Dover, with the railroad finally securing written contracts in 1860 from all shippers of freight to and from Canal Dover to use the railroad instead of the canal.[38] As many people saw it, the canals of Ohio were a definite liability. The wolves began to howl.

DISILLUSIONMENT AND LEASE, 1857–1861

In 1850 the Board of Public Works bypassed the legislature with its discretionary administrative powers and ordered extensive repairs on the canals, including the rebuilding of 19 locks on the Ohio Canal. In 1851, the board proposed to the legislature that, in order to meet railroad competition, the state should undertake a major program of reconstruction, including enlarging and deepening Ohio's canals. The program would have cost a little over $2 million. The legislature turned down the canal modernization as well as similar requests that followed.[39]

As early as the session of 1852–53, a proposition was introduced into the state senate to dispose of the canals. The committee on public works made a favorable report on the proposal, stating that the canals could be sold for $4 million. No action was taken on this bill, but both the legislature and the people of Ohio began thinking in terms of ridding themselves of the burden of maintaining the canals. At first, a few of the least profitable and useful of the public works were disposed of. The Warren County Canal, a small branch on the southern portion of the Miami & Erie, was sold in 1854, and a portion of the National Road between Springfield and Bridgeport was leased.

In an attempt to reduce the annual maintenance costs of the state's canals, the legislature, in 1855, bowing to the prevalent thought that "private enterprise is more efficient," signed a five-year contract with private firms for maintenance and repairs of the canals. This plan was a failure from the beginning. Rather than demonstrating the efficiency of private enterprise, the contractors neglected all but emergency repairs to maintain their own profits. As a result, the canals became nearly impass-able in many sections during 1856. Banks collapsed, culverts and locks deteriorated, and vegetation clogged reservoirs, feeder channels, and the main canal itself. The legislature cut the board's budget so sharply that even adequate supervision of the contractors proved impossible.

The legality and worth of the canal maintenance contracts were debated furiously within the legislature and among the populace. The contracts were finally repudiated by the legislature in 1857 when a special commit- · tee discovered that fraud and collusion had occurred during the original negotiations. However, after the contract system had been nullified, the Board of Public Works continued to use four of the five contractors for maintenance work.

During the debate on the legality of the 1855 contracts, one strong faction of the legislature sought to rid the state of its canals altogether by outright sale to private interests. Opponents of that plan blocked it suc-cessfully, but by the late 1850s, disposal or retention of the public works became one of the principal questions in Ohio. In 1857, Ohio's Governor Chase recommended the sale of the canals for their "fair value." Later that year the state auditor placed a value of $3 million on them. A year later, due to decreasing tonnage and revenues, the estimate was reduced to $2 million. In 1859, the legislature passed an act that would allow the leasing of the entire public works for five years at $54,000 per year. Any leasing company was required to have a $510,000 bond, railroad companies were forbidden to bid, and rigid conditions of maintenance and repair were laid down. There were no bidders.[40]

Early in 1860, a firm proposed to lease the canals for 10 years (begin-ning May 16) for $200,000. The proposal included the promise to keep the canals in good repair and return them to the state in good condition. The company also agreed to purchase all the state's equipment at a fair appraisal and not to raise the tolls over those of 1858.[41] The legislature, however, was not yet ready to lease the canals, and that year it passed two acts designed to shave operating expenses on the canals. In March 1860, the Board of Public Works was directed to release all the men who had been acting as lock tenders along Ohio's canals, except for those stationed at feeder gates. The legislature also passed another act that month limiting expenditures on all the public works to $2,000 per month.[42]

The harvests of 1860 were good in Ohio. The canals might have shown a modest profit had not disastrous flooding in April caused great damage to the system. The through canal from Cleveland to Portsmouth wasn't opened until May 30, and the costs to repair the canals after these floods far exceeded the monthly maintenance allowance. Many in and out of the legislature decided that it now seemed desirable for the state to rid itself of such an expensive burden. The legislature applied itself to the problem and, on May 8, 1861, it passed an act providing for the lease of the public works for a period of 10 years to the highest bidder. Bids were advertised, two were received, and on June 2, 1861, the canals of Ohio passed into private hands.

Merwin Street Bridge in Cleveland in the 1870s facing south toward Sloop Lock 43. (David Meyer, canal historian)

Boat-level view from the canal looking north toward Harvard Street Bridge in Cleveland.

Peninsula Aqueduct and the Moody-Thomas Mill.

Cascade area in north Akron showing Lock 13 below the railroad trestle.

From Akron's Market Street Bridge facing south with Lock 8 in foreground.

A typical three-cabin freighter in Massillon just south of the Tremont Street Bridge.

Canada Mill above Lock 6 in Navarre.

A three-cabin freighter loaded with cordwood in Tuscarawas County and bound for a paper mill up north.

The *River Mills* from the New Philadelphia lateral.

Canal Dover and the Dover Hydraulic. Henry Howe, *Historical Collections of Ohio*, 1847.

Coal boat loading at Nick Heipert's mine in Trenton, Tuscarawas County.

Canal bridge and mine in Trenton, Tuscarawas County.

Village of Seventeen in Tuscarawas County, built around the mill and Lock 17. Note the pleasure boat *Mayflower* to the right of the state boat.

Roscoe Basin in Coshocton. (Courtesy of Louis Baus and Roscoe Village Foundation Photo files)

The *E. L. Lybakser*, an excursion boat, in the Walhonding Aqueduct, Coshocton County. (Courtesy of Louis Baus and Roscoe Village Foundation Photo files)

Aqueduct in Newark, Licking County.

A two-deck grain boat loading at Lancaster in Fairfield County on the Hocking Canal.

A houseboat near upper lock at Lockville on the Ohio Canal, Fairfield County. (Courtesy of David Meyer, canal historian)

The *George Watkins,* a two-deck grain boat, at Marfield Mills in Chillicothe. (Courtesy of David Meyer, canal historian)

Three Locks at Tomlinson's in Ross County.

Union Mills and Lock 50 at Portsmouth.

⊿ 3 ⊾
Administration and Finance

With the passing of the Canal Act of 1825 by the Ohio State Legislature, a Board of Canal Commissioners was created to administer to the construction of Ohio's canals. This act also authorized the creation of a canal fund, from which money would be disbursed as required to pay for the cost of constructing, maintaining, and operating the canals. The Canal Act handed over the administration of this fund to a Board of Canal Fund Commissioners.[1]

A three-man Board of Canal Commissioners had first been organized in 1822. Its task then was to supervise the work of the initial surveys. The board was made permanent in 1825 and its makeup increased from three members to seven. The governor appointed all seven and their terms of office were indeterminate. All were prominent in state politics, and nearly all had extensive business interests as well, so time spent serving the state was considered duty. Two of these men, Micajah Williams and Alfred Kelley, had been active in the original field surveys and were named acting commissioners.

Williams and Kelly were the actual superintendents of the canal project. Williams initially supervised work on the Miami Canal and Kelley on the northern division of the Ohio. Later, Williams moved over to assist on the southern division of the Ohio Canal. They had both left highly respected positions to perform this service for the princely salary of three dollars a day (with an extra dollar per day for expenses when

42

in the field).[2] Kelley, originally from the Cleveland area, was a lawyer and a state representative from Columbus when tapped to be a canal commissioner. Williams, also a lawyer, had dabbled in engineering in the Cincinnati area.

At their initial meeting in Columbus, the board set up an engineering corps for the fledgling canal system. They adapted a plan of organization that was a close copy of the system used in New York. A principal engineer headed the corps, advised the board on technical questions, and supervised work in the field. His salary was set at $2,000 per year plus expenses, nearly twice what the acting commissioners received. Resident engineers—whose responsibilities included laying out the line of the canal, preparing cost estimates, specifying contracts, and overseeing and estimating work done by contractors in the field—were appointed as necessary. The board set the salaries for them at three dollars a day while in the field. Senior assistant engineers were paid $45 per month, and junior assistant engineers and surveyors were paid $35 per month. The state engineering corps also employed rod-men, ax-men, and common laborers whose wages were calculated on a per diem or hourly basis.[3]

The Board of Canal Commissioners, a creation of the state legislature, reflected the desires of the people. During the late 1820s and into the late 1840s, Ohio citizens and the legislature favored the canals. Initially, when the construction phase of the canals took place in a location that the legislators were not familiar with, their control over the board's powers was marginal. The legislature did not give the Board of Canal Commissioners free rein, however. Technically, all decisions pertaining to Ohio's canals were the result of legislative acts. The state legislature also required that the Board of Canal Commissioners report to them annually about canal activities.[4]

Ohio's political climate in the 1820s was simple and uncluttered. At that time there were no strong political lobbyists or intrigue. That made the job of the board a bit easier. The Board of Canal Commissioners was a unique entity in the history of Ohio. Only in the mustering of men for the War of 1812 were so many people involved. Yet the canal project also involved millions of dollars to be spent in an efficient manner over a number of years. Fortunately for the citizens of Ohio, the men picked for the initial Board of Canal Commissioners were outstanding in their intelligence and zeal to build and perfect a statewide canal system. Not only did the commissioners have to supervise an operation of unprecedented proportions, but they had to do so in a manner that pleased the citizens along the canal route and appeased those who had been bypassed.

Disagreements about the priority of construction and whether new canals should be added to the system were common, even among board members. However, no matter how intense their differences were, the commissioners maintained a united front in public. This show of unity enhanced their standing as an impartial agency, and they earned a reputation for serving the best interests of the state, free of special local agendas.

One of the board's most onerous tasks was dealing with the seizure of private property for canal purposes. The Canal Act of 1825, under the law of eminent domain, had given the board power to seize any land, timber, stone, and so forth, required for the construction of the canals. Many property owners willingly donated materials or land, or sold them without objection. Others, however, did object to confiscation or contested the prices offered. In such cases, the Canal Act provided for binding arbitration by three-man boards of appraisers appointed by the canal commissioners and usually composed of leading citizens from the local area. The decisions of the appraisal boards could be appealed only to the state legislature.[5] Later, when the canals were not of primary use, there were many claims that the state originally "entered upon and appropriated the land wanted without any sort of preliminary procedure," and "if a farmer made complaint, he was told that he would be benefited by the canal more than he would be damaged."[6]

Initially, the Board of Canal Commissioners firmly resisted all efforts to expand the canal system. They were aware of the state's precarious financial position and firmly believed that the initial system of canals should be finished and earning revenues before any additions were built. However, the Canal Act of 1825 had guaranteed that the Miami Canal would be extended to Lake Erie at an early date.

John Johnston, who had extensive land holdings along the route of the proposed extension, was appointed to fill a vacancy on the Board of Canal Commissioners in 1828. He immediately began lobbying quietly among board members for quick authorization of the extension. The first extension to the Miami Canal was authorized by the legislature in 1828, with construction beginning in 1831. The first expansion of the Ohio Canal was a two-mile branch from Webbsport to the Muskingum River at Dresden. This branch, the Muskingum Sidecut, was also authorized in 1828. It provided communication between the Ohio Canal and the Muskingum River and was opened for navigation by September 1830.[7]

Micajah Williams and Alfred Kelley both resigned as acting canal commissioners in 1833, and though Kelley remained as a board member for a few years, the tone of the board was changing. By 1836, the state's political parties saw the canal commission (and its many appointments) as something that should be reformed to give the party in power more positions to distribute as favors and rewards.

Sentiment for reforming the canal board administration on a "spoils" basis reached a high point in March 1836, the same year the legislature approved a massive expansion of the public works. The Democratic admin- istration in Columbus replaced the Board of Canal Commissioners with a Board of Public Works. This board consisted of six members appointed by joint resolution of the legislature. Two were to be acting commissioners at a salary of $1,500 per year; the other four were advisory commissioners and were paid on a per diem basis for attending board meetings. The state was divided into four districts, and one advisory commissioner was appointed from each district. Three commissioners were to be appointed each year, with each member serving two years. The effects of the 1836 reorganiza- tion, and the new projects authorized, enlarged the board's discretionary power in approving construction of new works. This reorganization also introduced the concept of geographic representation and injected party politics into the administration of the public works.[8]

Early Finance, 1825–1836

To ensure the honest and efficient handling of the finances of canal construction, a Board of Canal Fund Commissioners was created. It was to be solely in charge of raising and disbursing the funds necessary to build Ohio's canals. The state of Ohio in 1825 was a frontier area, rich in promise but poor in cash. Ohio could not finance the proposed canal system from its current treasury, nor could its citizens be expected to pay for it through taxation. Therefore, a rather complex method of financing the canals using a number of income sources was employed.

Loans, bond issues with the authorized faith and credit of the state of Ohio behind them, were the predominant source of funding during the early construction phase of the Ohio Canal. An initial loan of $400,000 at 5 percent was issued in 1825 and another for $1 million at 6 percent in 1826. These were followed by loans for $1.2 million in 1827, $1.2 million in 1828, $300,000 in 1830, and $100,000 in 1832. All the later loans were at 6 percent interest, to be redeemed "at the pleasure of the State between 1850 and 1875, at such time as the Canal Fund Commissioners should determine."[9]

In order to retire the interest and principal on these loans, the state had pledged all net proceeds or tolls collected on the canals, all water rentals and other profits connected with the canals, $40,000 of the money then in the state treasury, $30,000 of the revenue to be raised in 1825, and revenue raised from specific canal taxation.[10] The state legislature and the canal fund commissioners were reluctant to resort to taxation to retire the canal bonds until all other sources were used. One of these sources was the "borrowing" of the school fund and several other funds that were accumulating in the state treasury. The canal fund commissioners borrowed three of these funds in 1827 (they were then paid back at year's end at 6 percent interest). The same thing was done in 1828 and 1829. In 1830, a fourth fund was added. In March 1831, the legislature passed an act "by which all monies belonging to the common school fund were to be applied to defray the expenses of constructing the canals until they were completed."[11]

Revenue from the state's loans provided a minor source of income. While in various New York and Ohio banks awaiting disbursement for construction costs, these loans earned nearly $150,000 in interest up to 1834. Some of the loans issued in the late 1820s and early 1830s were sold at premiums and then added to the canal fund. On May 28, 1828, the U.S. Congress granted Ohio's request for federal lands to help finance the state's canals. Congress released more than 900,000 acres of government lands (mostly in the western portion of the state) to be sold to assist in Ohio's canal construction. Most of the money generated from government land sales, however, went to pay for the cost of Ohio's western canal extensions after 1831. Of course there was also the canal tax, paid directly to the canal fund commissioners from 1826 through 1846.[12]

All money entering the canal fund was first placed in a New York City bank. As funds were required for the payment of work done, the canal fund commissioners remitted the money to the Ohio banks that had been designated as official disbursing agents. The deposited funds could be withdrawn only by an acting canal commissioner to pay a specific contractor for work finished.

Ordinarily, the engineer in charge of the work made monthly inspections, which included certifying the name of the contractor, the type of work done, and how much work had been done. These monthly checks were cashed at an official state bank by the engineer in charge, and the contractor was paid in cash as the job progressed. The final payment, sometimes minus a "performance bond" that was paid after the job had proven its worth, was made when the entire job was finished.

The same method of payment by check, initially authorized by the acting canal commissioner, was used for land purchases, damage claims, and salaries of the engineering staff. By this system, no money actually passed through the hands of the acting canal commissioners, and fraud was only possible with the connivance of all three of the participants—the acting canal commissioner, the engineer, and the contractor.[13]

ADMINISTRATION, 1837–1861

The Whigs regained control of the state legislature in 1837 and immediately attacked the reorganization of the canal board, charging the Democratic board members with incompetency and negligence. They demanded reform, and in March 1838, the legislature disestablished the Board of Public Works and created a new agency with an old name, the Canal Commission. This new commission consisted of four full-time members (three Whigs and one Democrat) who were engineers with long records of state service. Geographic representation was not an official provision to appointment, but each of the four commissioners came from a different region of the state.

A year later, Democrats gained control of the legislature. They immediately legislated the Canal Commission out of existence and reestablished the Board of Public Works. This time the board contained five members, all full-time officers, but the district representation system was not revived. In 1840 the legislature reduced the board to four members and in 1842 to three. Then, aside from periodic changes of the board members themselves due to political changes in the legislature, the makeup of the Board of Public Works remained virtually unchanged through the decades of the 1840s and 1850s.[14]

One fact is now obvious: the high quality of administration that was so prevalent in the early years of Ohio's canals was missing in the "reformed" Board of Public Works. The legislature and Ohio citizens leveled many claims of incompetence and poor engineering at the board during the late 1830s and the decade of the 1840s. Some of these accusations may have been true, though successive investigations failed to turn up any proof of actual wrongdoing. Also, the legislature held some of the blame for the inefficiencies of the late 1830s and 1840s. It placed more and more political pressure on the performance of the board during the financial panics of the period and at the same time reduced salaries, forcing experienced engineers and administrators out of service. Reduced maintenance fund authorizations also strained the physical limitations of the canals.

During this period, political patronage became an established practice in selecting Board of Public Works personnel. As a result, occasionally incompetent personnel caused engineering and administrative mistakes in judgment. The new state constitution, adopted in 1851, provided for the annual popular election of members of the Board of Public Works. This marked the final step in the absorption of the Public Works into the mechanism of political patronage.

Unfortunately, the poor record of efficiency and administration of the Public Works during this period, justified or not by the country's economic woes, resulted in a complete loss of public confidence in the integrity of the administration. That, in turn, led to a general disillusionment of the state's citizens with public enterprise. By the early 1850s, Ohioans began to believe that any major project built and run by the state would involve excessive costs and be staffed by political hacks.[15]

FINANCE, 1837–1861

Though the Ohio & Erie Canal was technically completed from Cleveland to Portsmouth some four years before the 1836 expansion authorization, two of the branches authorized in the expansion were potentially important feeders to that canal. Also, revenues from the Ohio Canal were funneled back into the system to finance the entire expansion project. Therefore, the financial manipulations of the commissioners during this period are of extreme importance to the history of the Ohio Canal.

Until March 1837, when the passage of the Loan (or Plunder) Law pledged the credit of the state to private improvement companies, Ohio's public works were constructed and maintained with unsurpassed economy and skill. By January 1833, for example, the state had a fully operational Ohio Canal and navigable branches, which were more than 330 miles long and which cost slightly over $5 million to construct.[16]

The expansion program of 1836 and the Loan Law the next year placed a tremendous additional burden on the state's finances. The financial panics that began in 1837 and continued nearly unabated until the mid-1840s stretched those resources to the breaking point. The canal fund commissioners, "after great exertion," were able to sell only $339,073 of 6 percent stock in New York in 1839. They were able to "dispose" of an additional $760,000 worth of bonds in London.

The loan act was repealed on March 17, 1840, but Ohio's debt had been increased significantly. Then, in the early 1840s, eight states, including Pennsylvania and Maryland, defaulted on the interest payments of their debts. Several states actually repudiated their entire debt. As a result, credit in all "western" states was seriously reduced, and Ohio found it impossible to sell any loan outside the state in 1840. The commissioners distributed circulars describing the status of the existing canals and the requirements for additional funds among banks throughout Ohio. The response was a very generous $500,000 loan which was enough to carry on the work for that year.

In 1841, the canal fund commissioners estimated that it would require an additional $2.4 million to complete the expanded canal system as authorized in 1836. The legislature appropriated $2.3 million for the public works but left it to the canal fund commissioners to find the funds to borrow. They were able to effect temporary loans of $275,000 in New York and $133,000 in London. The commissioners again went to state banks to obtain the rest of the needed funds. Only two banks responded this time—the Bank of Chillicothe and the Franklin Bank of Columbus. The total sum was for only $1.08 million, but the commissioners were able to continue work on the canals for the remainder of 1841.[17]

The year 1842 was a dark one for the men handling Ohio's canal financing. Failure of the wheat crop within the state, coupled with severe competition from the steamboat river trade, reduced canal tolls to below that required to pay even the interest on the current loans. Some $1.36 million was required to pay current estimates for work done and work yet to be completed. Checks to canal contractors issued by state banks were being discounted at 40 to 50 percent due to fears that Ohio, like its neighboring states, would default on its loans. A payment of $500,000 in bonds, based on government lands still held by the state, was offered to contractors on the Miami Extension and Wabash & Erie Canals. Only $350,816 worth of bonds was accepted. An act early in 1842 suspended all work on Ohio's internal improvements other than the Wabash & Erie Canal. Branches, such as the truncated Ohio Canal Branch and the Walhonding, remained foreshortened and unproductive. All that the commissioners attempted to do from then on was to complete the unfinished work and to pay off the debt already piled up. This proved to be a much greater task than was first estimated. The canal fund commissioners managed to sell $1,546,800 worth of bonds that year in New York and London, but, due to fears about Ohio's credit, they were sold at discount and netted only $1,026,735.[18]

An act on March 13, 1843, provided for an issue of $1.5 million of 7 percent bonds, redeemable in 1851 and not to be sold under par. When two of the canal fund commissioners traveled to New York to negotiate the loan, they found previous issues of 6 percent Ohio bonds selling at 69½ percent to 70 percent of par. Soon this fell to 66½ percent. The commissioners published a pamphlet detailing the state's current financial condition, a brief history of the public works, and the cost of construction, repairs, and the like. They then issued a notice offering the 7 percent bonds. A single offer for them was made, agreeing to take $600,000 at par, with an option of subscribing for the remaining $900,000 by September 15. The state's credit was saved. The influx of this money was felt immediately along the unfinished canal lines and throughout the state. From this point on, Ohio's credit grew as local and national economies rebounded. There were only two small final sales of bonds during the next two years, a 6 percent loan for $210,000 in 1844 and another for $100,000 in 1845.[19]

The governor declared in his message of 1846 that "the public improvements undertaken by the state are now fully completed." The state debt at that time was a whopping $19,301,252. This debt, added to from time to time for outstanding expenses (particularly during the Civil War), was not retired until 1903, but the last charge for Ohio's public involvement in canals, roads and railroads was made in 1845.[20]

Administration and Finance during the Lease, 1861–1877

During the 16-plus years the public works were leased to a private company, the administration, from the state's standpoint, differed very little from what it had been prior to the lease. The Board of Public Works was maintained and the yearly reports continued to be presented to the legislature. Now, though, a general agent appointed by the lessees was the liaison between the board and the leasing company. When maintenance was required, the engineer representing the board recommended items to be repaired to the general agent and the company would comply. The method for achieving the repair, however, was up to the company. That meant the solution was usually efficient, cost-effective, and generally short-term.

Financing during the lease is a murky area. Few formal records are available. The legislature still paid the salaries for the board members and any engineers working for the board. Theoretically, the leasing company handled all additional expenses. The fact was, in some cases, the legislature was still required to authorize and furnish funds for canal projects. When the lessees felt that the board recommended a project that constituted original work and not general maintenance, the company would refuse to perform the required tasks unless funded by a legislative act.[21]

Administration after the Lease, 1878–1912

When the lessees surrendered the canals late in 1877, an appointed receiver ran them from December 1, 1877, to May 15, 1878, at a cost of $45,299. Earnings during this period amounted to $69,766. The Board of Public Works was reorganized by an act of May 14, 1878, and took charge of the remaining state canals the next day. The Board of Public Works now consisted of three members and a chief engineer. The three members each received a yearly salary of $800 and were elected for three years. The chief engineer, appointed by the governor, ran the organization and received a salary of $2,000 per year.[22] The first chief engineer appointed was William J. Jackson, a former lessee of Ohio's public works.

In 1888 Governor Foraker appointed a three-man canal survey commission to determine what canal lands the state owned. All the major state canals were surveyed between 1890 and 1892. The commission, initially consisting of three members, was reduced to two in 1892. The state did not have clear titles to much of the canal lands claimed in the surveys since much of it had been acquired by eminent domain, donation, purchase, gifts, and grants. Determining just what the state did own was an important and difficult task. Few original maps or documents existed, and much of the commission's information came from testimony of events that had occurred more than 50 years earlier. The commission discovered many serious cases of encroachment of canal lands and began a program of reclaiming what lands it could. At that time formal deeds were initiated, placing the state as owner of canal lands where there had been no owner before. It was at this time that the state legalized its occupation of the canal lands.[23]

When the canal lands were vacated for navigational purposes in later years, many landowners believed that the canal lands would revert back to them, but deeds initiated by the commission in the late 1890s held up in court. The canal commission was abolished in 1906, though its duties were far from over. The remaining work was transferred to the Board of Public Works.[24]

In 1898 the legislature designated the Loramie Reservoir on the Miami & Erie Canal as a public lake to be called Indian Lake. This policy was expanded to the Licking and Portage Reservoirs on the Ohio Canal by an act in 1902.[25] A 1911 act virtually abandoned the Ohio Canal, including what remained of the Hocking branch, below the Dresden Sidecut to the southern terminus at Portsmouth (except for a hydraulic in Newark). That same act designated several of the large public lake reservoirs as state park lands and set up a separate park board to administer them. Then, on December 31, 1912, the state legislature officially abolished the Board of Public Works and replaced it with one person, a supervisor of public works.[26]

4
Operation of the Lease

LEASE, 1861–1877

The canals of Ohio were ostensibly leased to a company of six Ohioans on June 2, 1861. In actuality, the lease was held by a consortium of more than 20 men. When the Lease Bill first began working its way through the legislature, it became obvious that a number of "companies" were being formed to submit bids. In fact, as many as four different companies were ready to submit competitive bids, but because multiple bids would have driven up the cost of the lease, wiser heads prevailed. The men joined forces, formed two companies, and submitted two bids— one for $20,050 per year and the other for $20,075. The "high" bid won. When the winning company, consisting of six front men, received the lease, 15 additional shares were sold within a couple of days to men who had been promised a portion of the action. Each of the shareholders (or bondsmen, as they called themselves) initially anteed up $1,000 to cover the lease bond. They spent about another $1,000 for start-up equipment. At the end of each year, after the salaries of the president and an officer or two were paid, all remaining profits were divided equally among the bondsmen.[1]

All the bondsmen were canal men. Many had been involved in the maintenance contracts of 1855. Two of the three men who had formed a company in 1860 to lease the canals were bondsmen. All wanted to make a profit from the canals, but they also wanted to see the canals of Ohio remain a viable transportation system. The lessees organized quickly. By the end of June 1861, a general agent, secretary, and treasurer had been named. The general agent acted as liaison with the Board of Public Works. For supervision and repair purposes, the lessees divided Ohio's public works into nine divisions, including the Ohio, Walhonding, and Hocking Canals.[2]

The state's Board of Public Works and a small engineering staff were maintained. The board continued to deliver annual reports to the legislature and, during most years of the lease, the reports were complimentary, describing the cooperation of the lessees performing the routine canal maintenance. There were a couple of areas where they disagreed, however. In some cases, the lessees considered the requests by the board's engineers as "original work," not mere maintenance. In these instances, a legislative act authorizing expenditures was required before the lessees would perform the work. An article in a Cincinnati newspaper early in 1874 estimated that the state had authorized nearly $300,000 for canal projects up to that time.[3] Another area of disagreement, according to engineers' reports, was that the lessees' maintenance procedures were only a temporary fix and would not contribute to the longevity of the Ohio & Erie Canal.

The lessees implemented a number of money-saving practices for routine maintenance tasks. Each spring, the state had drained the canal channel and hired hordes of men with picks and shovels to clean out bars and obstructions. The lessees, however, constructed steam dredges that could clean out the channels without draining them. This money- and time-saving procedure was often augmented by dredging a narrow channel just wide enough to accommodate one boat for long stretches of canal. "Passing" places were fashioned every few miles. This procedure annoyed some boatmen and caused a few bottlenecks, but traffic was so light then that the minor delays were tolerated. To maintain a proper depth for fully loaded craft, canal banks and regulating channel tumbles were raised in places where this procedure was more economical than dredging.[4]

The lessees also developed an economical way to extend the life of a canal lock without completely rebuilding it. The most prevalent problem with older stone locks was that the surrounding earth pressed in the top few stone courses of the lock, making it too narrow for boats to negotiate. The lessees chipped back enough of the inner stone walls of the upper courses to place wooden stringers. They then nailed interior, watertight planking to the stringers and placed grout in the spaces on either side of the stringers (between the planking and remaining stone wall).[5]

In general, the lessees managed to keep the canal in relatively good condition. The dry years of 1872 and 1873 resulted in shallow channels and boats of more than 3 feet 3 inches draft so that they occasionally bottomed out in certain sections. That resulted in bad publicity from the boatmen, but by 1874 and 1875, with the benefit of more rain and judicious dredging, loaded boats with drafts up to 4½ feet could regularly navigate the upper reaches of the Ohio Canal.[6]

The lessees also performed more conventional repairs and rebuilds on canal structures, though many of the larger jobs were with legislative funds. At least one stone lock (Lock 13 at Lockville in Fairfield County) was entirely rebuilt during the lessees' reign (1862). The feeder dams at the Black Hand Narrows in Licking County and at Circleville in Pickaway County were rebuilt in 1867 following devastating floods the previous year. The lessees took special measures to ensure quick transit of freight through the Ohio Canal. In order to minimize a bottleneck just south of the Licking Summit, the lessees maintained several "lighters" (flat-bottom scows) to off-load cargo and pass them through areas of low water during dry seasons.[7]

Noticeably absent from the Board of Public Works' annual reports was any mention of the tonnage carried or activity maintained on the canals during the lease. Isolated figures and information gleaned from local newspapers and later interviews with individual bondsmen indicate that, though traffic for 1861 was a bit slow, it picked up considerably over the next several years. This was due particularly to the outbreak of the Civil War in 1861 and the demand from the East for Ohio grain. With the railroads busy transporting war materiel, canal transportation was a necessity. The boatyards on the northern division of the Ohio Canal, at Akron, Peninsula, and Boston, were near capacity shortly after the outbreak of the war. Between 1862 and 1863, these three towns alone built 16 or 18 boats. In addition, many older boats were refurbished. Local papers acknowledged the increased freight caused by the war effort but attributed most of the increased canal traffic to the "efficiency of private enterprise."[8] During these flush war years, the lease appears to have been a profitable enterprise. The bondsmen each earned up to $5,000 yearly, after expenses, for the first four or five years of the lease, though the *Cincinnati Commercial,* in a January 1874 article highly critical of the lessees, estimated that each of the 25 bondsmen (there were actually 23) had made a profit of $75,000 over the first 12 years of the lease.[9]

During the spring of 1866, however, major floods in eastern Ohio destroyed large portions of the Ohio Canal. The lessees quickly made the necessary repairs and petitioned the legislature to extend the lease, even though the present one wouldn't expire for another four years. The lease was extended at the same annual fee until 1881. Though a few formal freight lines were operating at the initiation of the lease in 1861, more and more tonnage on the Ohio Canal was concentrated on hauling coal from the mines along the Hocking Branch Canal and from mines along the northern division in Summit, Stark, and Tuscarawas Counties to industries north along the canal and to Lake Erie. As time passed, most of these short, specialized hauls fell to independent freighters, often operated only by a captain and two or three helpers.[10] During the summer of 1872, many of these independent boatmen banded together to unilaterally raise the freight rates on coal. The mine owners objected and the boatmen pulled their boats up and refused to work. This strike lasted less than a week before the coal mine operators gave in and the strike was averted, but railroad company agents in the area began gathering like buzzards.[11]

With state inspectors at a minimum and the canals no longer under direct state control, many nearby landowners took advantage of the situation and began fencing in land right up the edge, or even the center, of the towpath and up to the water's edge on the berm bank. An appeal to the legislature for stricter laws was made, but during the lease period, the state legislature operated as if the canals did not even exist. Important portions of the state's canal system were abandoned by acts of the legislature between 1861 and the termination of the lease in 1877. The southern terminal facilities of the Miami & Erie Canal in Cincinnati were abandoned in 1863. The northern terminal facilities of the same canal in Toledo were abandoned the next year. In this latter case new terminal facilities were provided, but in both cases the abandoned canal lands were quickly transferred to railroad interests.

The state sold its one-third interest in the Pennsylvania & Ohio Canal, a private waterway connecting Pennsylvania's canal system with that of Ohio at Akron, to the Cleveland & Mahoning Railroad in 1863. After gaining control of the canal, the railroad increased tolls to such an extent that P&O traffic fell off drastically, and that important feeder to the Ohio Canal became inoperative after 1868. The lower seven miles of the Hocking Canal at Carroll, from Chauncy to Athens, was abandoned in 1873 after severe spring floods destroyed that section of the canal. The state abandoned another seven miles of the canal in 1876, from Lock 21 below Nelsonville to Chauncy. Large tonnages of coal from the mines of the Hocking Valley were lost by the Ohio Canal when this important branch was foreshortened.[12]

The city of Cleveland purchased the northernmost three miles of canal, including the important terminal facilities adjacent to Lake Erie. Strangely, even though the transfer was legalized by a legislative act, the lessees received the $125,000 "fee" from the city of Cleveland.[13] The legal transference of these lands took place in 1873. However, the city was required to construct outlet and weigh locks at the new northern end of the canal. The new locks weren't operational until the beginning of the 1878 boating season. From then on, boatmen wishing to transship cargo to lake vessels had to negotiate a dangerous four-mile stretch of the Cuyahoga River, usually as part of a tug float. The next year, the city of Cleveland leased this valuable terminal site to the Valley Railroad for 99 years.[14] Then in 1878 the Scioto Valley Railroad began construction along the southern portion of the Ohio Canal, effectively draining passenger and express traffic from that portion of the canal.[15]

Largely as a result of abandoned canal segments, loss of public confidence, continued railroad competition, and several extremely dry years, tonnage and traffic fell significantly on the Ohio & Erie Canal during the mid-1870s. Testimonies from individual bondsmen in 1875 indicated that the annual dividends on their investment hadn't reached $3,000 "for the last seven years."[16]

Competition of the railroads drew business from the canals, but almost as important was the disorganization of traffic arrangements on the canals themselves. The formal transportation lines that had controlled canal business were gradually dissolved during the last few years of the lease. Boats ran wild, so their trips became uncertain and potential shippers could not rely on them.[17]

The lessees announced in June 1877 that they would not pay the final installment on their lease, due December 1. They reasoned that the lease had been broken when the city of Hamilton, on the Miami & Erie Canal, filled up a portion of the town's basin (which was permitted by an act of April 14, 1877). The lessees formally abandoned their lease on December 1, 1877. Receivers were appointed to administer the public works until the state resumed control.[18]

STATE OPERATION, 1878–1902

A legislative act of May 14, 1878, returned control of Ohio's canals to a reorganized Board of Public Works. A new position of chief engineer was created, and the first man to hold the governor-appointed position was William J. Jackson of Piqua. Jackson had been one of the original lessees, and the style of short-term maintenance performed during the lease was continued during his term. Locks repaired by the plank-and-grout method were replanked, and new gates were hung at many of the locks. Jackson stated in his first annual report to the legislature that "it affords me the highest satisfaction to be able to report that the Public Works of the state are in good repair and first class condition for business." He added in his 1879 report that the Ohio Canal, the Hocking Canal, and the Muskingum River Improvement were "in splendid working condition."[19]

The signs were there, however, forecasting a bleak future for the Ohio Canal. The southern portion, hampered by a poor water supply and a cumbersome terminus with the Ohio River, sometimes went "months without seeing a boat." The state legislature authorized Pike County commissioners to construct a gravel road on the canal's towpath from Waverly to the Scioto County Line.[20] There were even troubling signs along the northern portion of the Ohio Canal. The mines in Summit and Stark Counties began closing as the veins petered out, forcing boatmen to go into Tuscarawas and Coshocton Counties or to the Hocking Valley for cargoes.[21] Still, there was money to be made boating along that section of the canal if a man was willing to work hard and if the canal didn't get "out of fix" too often. Unfortunately, the short-range fixes, used since 1861, eventually deteriorated to the point where a complete and expensive rebuild of the canal's physical facilities was required. It was in the early 1880s that the state initiated the practice of assigning a section of the canal and a boat to a maintenance team that would travel to troubled areas and make repairs. This was the fourth type of craft on the canal—the state boat—and since it was assigned to a specific locality, it didn't require a center cabin for a spare team, as did the three-cabin freighter.[22]

The chief engineers who succeeded Jackson unanimously blamed the general decline of canal traffic and revenue on the lessees neglecting the canals' conditions. In truth, the canals of Ohio should have been completely refurbished and expanded during the 1850s in order to compete and survive. Instead, the legislature almost ignored them, cutting maintenance expenditures to a minimum. The canals were in a state of neglect when leased, but the lessees managed to patch the system together and make it run fairly well for nearly 20 years. If the Ohio canals required rebuilding and refurbishing in the 1850s, one can only imagine what condition they were in during the 1880s.

John B. Gregory succeeded Jackson as chief engineer in 1880 and promptly petitioned the federal government to conduct a survey for a modern, enlarged canal between the lake and river. The act of June 14, 1880, which granted Gregory's request, included a number of surveys in other areas but was underfunded. Results of the survey were slow in coming. The report, when finally made in 1884, proposed a ship canal between Delaware Creek on Lake Erie in the western part of the state and Mill Creek near Cincinnati. The estimated cost of a canal this size was $28,440,275. The report, making no recommendations, simply stated that a ship canal of the dimensions specified was feasible. Frank Snyder, chief engineer, was extremely pessimistic about obtaining the necessary funding for the proposed enlargement. Instead, he recommended in his 1885 report that the Miami & Erie Canal and that portion of the Ohio & Erie from Dover to Cleveland be leased and the remainder of Ohio's canals be sold. No action was taken.[23]

Severe floods devastated the lower portion of the Ohio Canal in 1882 and 1884, breaking the banks, filling the channel with debris, and destroying dams and other structures. The cost of repairing the damage far outstripped the meager legislative allocations that had been made for maintenance, so additional appropriations had to be made. While being repaired, the canal was shut down. To minimize the amount of traffic that transferred to competing railroad lines, the Board of Public Works lowered canal tolls. Even so, a great deal of traffic did jump to the railroads without returning. That loss, coupled with lower tolls, caused total canal receipts to fall drastically.[24]

For the next several years, as canal traffic continued to drop, Ohio's canal system slowly disintegrated due to the cession and abandonment of its various parts. The Muskingum River Improvement was ceded to the federal government in 1887. The upper portion of the Hocking Canal was leased to the Columbus, Hocking Valley, and Athens Railroad Company for 99 years. The state abandoned all but the lower six miles of the Walhonding Canal in 1896 after unsuccessfully attempting for many years to sell it to a railroad.[25]

The Federal Rivers and Harbors Act of 1894 gave the Ohio Board of Public Works another chance to interest the federal government in surveying a route for a ship canal through Ohio connecting Lake Erie and the Ohio River. The dimensions of the proposed canal were 70 feet wide at the waterline and 7 feet deep. Proposed locks were 150 feet by 21 feet, with a capacity for vessels that could carry at least 250 tons. Three routes through Ohio were considered—western, central, and eastern. The eastern route was to follow the route of the Ohio Canal south from Cleveland to Dresden and the Muskingum River to Marietta. The Akron Summit was to be lowered 9 feet to increase the water capacity of the Portage Lakes Reservoirs, and a new reservoir was to be constructed on the Cuyahoga River near Kent. The eastern route was to have 775 feet of lockage and cost an estimated $12.3 million. This eastern route would have been the most economical to construct. However, the survey report did not recommend constructing a canal along any of the three proposed routes, stating that there didn't appear to be sufficient benefit of interstate commerce from such a waterway and that constructing a canal along any of the proposed routes was "not advisable." It was up to the state of Ohio, then, to decide what to do with the remainder of its canal system.[26]

A new terminus at Portsmouth was finally completed in 1887, but traffic was nearly nonexistent by then along the southern portion of the Ohio & Erie Canal. A severe flood hit the canal in 1898. It wasn't until late summer that the northern division was running again. The Raccoon Creek Aqueduct in Newark collapsed during that 1898 flood, and the canal north of the Licking Summit to the Dresden Sidecut became incapable of carrying traffic. The Raccoon Creek Aqueduct was rebuilt in 1902 but only to supply local industries with water; boat traffic did not resume. A flood on the lower Scioto that same year put an end to boating from Waverly to the south, though officially the canal was still open. In effect, the Ohio Canal was open only for commercial boating from Dresden to Cleveland, though an occasional craft would manage to get as far south from Cleveland as Roscoe or Dresden.[27]

Limited traffic was maintained in the northern portion of the canal, but there seemed to be few state efforts to support it. The constant rumors of the canal being closed, leased, sold, or just abandoned had an adverse effect on the few businesses that still depended on canal traffic. Many of them began looking for alternate transportation sources. It was obviously only a matter of time until the Ohio Canal ceased to exist. By the late 1890s, converted freighters, taking church and picnic groups on short jaunts to nearby picnic groves along the canal, were the most prevalent type of traffic on the canal.[28]

Attempted Rebuild, 1903–1910

Charles E. Perkins of Akron, a staunch supporter of rehabilitating and enlarging Ohio canals, was appointed chief engineer by Governor McKinley in 1892. After the disappointing report of the 1895 survey board, Perkins put all his energy into persuading the state to increase the depth of water in Ohio's existing canals to 5 feet to permit the use of boats of 100-ton capacity. Perkins's 1903 report became the bible for canal improvement. He reiterated his plea to dredge the canals to a 5-foot depth, but the clinching argument was his belief that existing structures didn't require rebuilding. Only slight and inexpensive improvements would be required for existing locks, aqueducts, and so forth. The Ohio & Erie Canal, he assured the legislature in his 1903 report, could be improved and rehabilitated from Cleveland to Dresden, where boats could use the federal Muskingum Improvement to the Ohio River, for a "mere" $573,186.33.[29]

The 1903 report also stated that rehabilitation of the canals was imperative if they were to continue to operate. In 1903, boats of 80-ton capacity could navigate from Cleveland to Trenton. With additional improvements, Perkins believed boats with 60-ton loads could navigate to Newcomerstown and those with 50-ton loads from Columbus to Waverly. The Ohio Canal below Waverly had been closed for a number of years.[30]

Ohio's legislators took Perkins's report to heart and on May 6, 1904, passed an act appropriating $75,000 in 1904 and $125,000 in 1905 for the reconstruction of the northern division of the Ohio & Erie Canal. The act provided for additional expenditures for a total of $573,186.33—the exact amount estimated in Perkins's 1903 report. The first of the appropriations was not to take effect until the Board of Public Works had negotiated new water leases of at least $30,000 per year for a minimum of five years. These leases were finalized by the end of 1904.

One problem with the rebuild budget was that Perkins's 1903 estimate of the cost was based on preliminary and, as it proved, incomplete and imperfect data. Coshocton Power and Light Company held a new waterpower lease, and the company expected to receive power from the Walhonding feeder, provided by a dam six miles up that waterway. Perkins's 1903 estimate had called for only minimal repairs to the dam, but, in light of the important waterpower lease, a new concrete dam was required to be constructed on the site of the original dam. [31]

Initial contracts to rebuild the canal were divided into three sections from Cleveland to Akron. A separate contract was made for the three locks on the Dresden Sidecut into the Muskingum River. This was an important contract, as the federal government had appropriated $100,000 for a dam and lock on the river between Zanesville and Dresden contingent on Ohio improving the connection of the sidecut with the Muskingum River.[32] Actual construction began near the end of the 1905 boating season, but another problem reared its head. With the Cleveland terminus cut off by construction in the canal, traffic ceased. An estimated 100 families were still making their living on the Ohio Canal in 1901. After 1905 or early 1906, the only boating possible on the northern division of the canal was south of Akron. A severe flood in the lower Tuscarawas Valley in March 1907 destroyed much of the canal and structures from Canal Dover to the south. This flood also tore out the big dam across the Scioto at Circleville, ending local boating through Chillicothe to Three Locks.[33]

After 1905 or 1906, all of those 100 canal families were out of work, awaiting the completion of the rebuild. Many boatmen sunk their boats in a convenient basin "for the duration." Others, anchored in a convenient widewater or next to a low bank, converted their craft into temporary living quarters. Both groups attempted to get temporary jobs in nearby factories until they could resume boating.[34]

Perkins had estimated that the locks and aqueducts could be refurbished with minimal effort and cost. The repairs were to be made with a relatively new engineering material, concrete. The problem with the locks was a familiar one: the top few courses of stone pressed into the lock chamber. The initial solution was to blow off the top courses with dynamite and rebuild the upper portions of the locks with formed concrete. So many other parts of the lock needed repair, however, that the revised solution was to chip back the original stone (except for the bottom few courses) some 10 to 12 inches and reform the interior with concrete. This proved to be overly time consuming. Therefore, the engineers' solution was to tear out the old lock completely and rebuild it with formed concrete, using some of the old stone as aggregate.

The rework dragged on from 1906 through 1909. The last few businesses along the canal found other means of transportation to receive materials and fuel and to ship their goods. Only in that section between Akron and the amusement parks on the shore of Summit Pond (now Summit Lake) was there any boat activity. A small fleet of steam launches and gas boats trundled patrons from the city of Akron to and from the beaches and fun of Summit Lake.[35]

The boatyard at Akron and the one in Canal Fulton stayed in business as a direct result of these craft. The remaining boatyards and other establishments that had catered to boatmen found other customers or closed up. Many of those 100 canal families found that living as a "Town Jake" wasn't that bad. They all worked hard, and many excelled in life away from the canal.

The total expenditure on the Ohio Canal refurbishment through 1909 was $790,000. Perkins's 1909 report estimated that another $243,600 would be required to finish the work to Dresden. Additional expenses had cropped up everywhere, and some of the work done had proven defective. Deep Lock 27 in Summit County showed signs of sagging concrete forms and had to be extensively repaired by state forces. Several contractors failed to wash the gravel aggregate going into the concrete and instead just scooped up what stones were available along the river banks. This resulted in understrength concrete and failed structures that slipped by the inspectors. They had to be rebuilt at state expense. Charges of fraud and mismanagement were leveled against the canal system's chief engineer.[36]

No appropriations were made for refurbishment of the Ohio Canal after 1909. The structures below Lower Trenton Lock 16 through Lower Adam's Mills Lock 30 had not been repaired. Reworking the Walhonding

Aqueduct had not been in Perkins's original estimate, yet it was part of the to-be-completed list in his 1909 report. The wooden towpath along the aqueduct's trough had been removed by state forces as a safety precaution in 1907, and the condition of the remaining structure in 1909 was "precarious."

Perkins's ninth consecutive term of office expired in May 1910. He was not reappointed; nor was he immediately replaced. There was no chief engineer's report to the legislature for 1910, and for several months the Ohio Canal was in a state of limbo.[37]

5

The Flood

John I. Miller was appointed chief engineer of Public Works on July 3, 1911. The canals of Ohio were, according to his first report, "in such a state of physical disability as to make it possible for navigation only in a very few instances." Miller referred to the previous regime only once when he said, "The fact that there has been mismanagement in the past is not the fault of the canals." He also urged that the canals be "put back into first-class condition for navigation in the near future. Miller's report further stated that "the Ohio & Erie Canal from Cleveland to Dresden has been rebuilt for most of the way, but the fact that there is no aqueduct at Roscoe, and that the dredging was discontinued at Tuscarawas [Trenton] on account of lack of funds, puts the whole system out of commission."[1]

In actuality, during the enforced hiatus of canal traffic during the attempted rebuild, the few mills, mines, and industries that had regularly shipped and received by canal either shifted their businesses elsewhere or were forced out of business. The boatmen, too, drifted away and into other jobs and lives. Only those few boats that had been dragged up onto shore alongside basins or widewaters and converted into homes survived.[2]

Mixed signals came from the legislature and the Board of Public Works regarding the future of the Ohio Canal. Major physical improvements were made along the canal in Cleveland, Akron, and Tuscarawas County as late as 1912. However, the "spoil" from dredging the canal channel south of Clinton in Summit County to the Stark County line had been left there in heaps, obstructing the towpath. The dredging spoil south of Clinton through Canal Fulton was not plowed smooth and leveled until 1912. Also, it seems that the portion of the canal through Navarre in Stark County to the Zoar feeder in Tuscarawas County was never refilled with water after the rebuild of New Lock 5A and the Cemetery Run Culvert south of Massillon in 1909.[3]

Meanwhile, the state busied itself with disposing of the lower portion of the Ohio Canal. Most of the canal line between the Dresden Sidecut in Muskingum County and Portsmouth was officially abandoned in 1911. Only the section between the Licking Summit Reservoir (Buckeye Lake) and a few industries in Newark remained, and those were for hydraulic purposes.

The remainder of the Ohio Canal was allowed to just exist. Then, on December 31, 1912, perhaps acting on the premise that they no longer considered Ohio canals as viable transportation systems, the state legislature abolished the three-man Board of Public Works and replaced it with a one-man supervisor of Public Works.[4] The legislature appointed John Miller as supervisor, which perhaps meant the state wasn't quite ready to give up on its canals. Even so, things were soon taken out of the legislature's hands.

The snows were heavy in Ohio during January and February of 1913. Then a rare early thaw occurred in mid-March, and on March 23, Easter Sunday, it began to rain. The rain continued as a heavy downpour all over the state. By the wee hours of Tuesday morning, the creeks and rivers throughout Ohio were at a record flood stage.[5] Though western Ohio was hardest hit, the rivers in eastern Ohio, including the Cuyahoga, Muskingum, Licking, and Scioto—rivers whose valleys carried the channel of the Ohio & Erie Canal—all experienced record flood stages.

The rain had begun falling in eastern Ohio around noon on Easter. More than eight inches fell during the next four days. Families in the Tuscarawas, Muskingum, and Cuyahoga River Valleys fled their homes. Cities in the valleys were without power, shelter, food, and water, and firemen could not reach fires.

The Tuscarawas River bottoms, including the canal near Clinton and Warrick, were covered by water for a width of 12 miles. All that water had to be funneled through the valley that contained Canal Fulton, Massillon, and Navarre. The Tuscarawas River overflowed its banks at Canal Fulton and, together with the canal, raced through town. All the wood stocked in inventory at the McLaughlin boatyard just below the town was swept downriver. Later, the boatyard's owner, Charles McLaughlin, found much of his stock along the river banks far below town, but when he attempted to retrieve it, he was driven off by an armed landowner who demanded McLaughlin "prove the lumber was his." Charles McLaughlin closed his boatyard as did most of the remaining canal-based businesses.[6]

Easter Sunday, March 23, had seen the residents of Massillon going to special musical church services through a driving rain. The rain continued all day and night Monday. At 8:45 on the morning of Tuesday, March 25, the rising Tuscarawas River passed the previous high-water mark set in 1904 and kept increasing at the rate of two feet per hour. Only the roofs of the homes along the canal were above water.

At 11:00 A.M. the only two schools in Massillon that had managed to open were closed. The raging Tuscarawas waters, reaching halfway up the sides of a house on Tremont, battered and shoved until the house rose from its foundation and floated off, only to crash against a railroad trestle across the canal and disintegrate.

Rising waters covered the Ohio Drilling Company, the Massillon Foundry, and the Schuster Brewery to a depth of three to four feet. Part of the Sippo Creek Culvert under South Erie Street collapsed, and the creek flooded the main business section of Massillon. The chief of police called for all Massillon saloon owners to close, and most complied, but several drunken men were pulled out of the floodwaters of downtown Massillon by police. Tuesday afternoon, when the flood was at its height, acting Mayor Koontz issued a proclamation forbidding looting and destruction of property.[7]

The three villages that made up Navarre were on high ground and didn't suffer badly, though the canal through Navarre was utterly destroyed. Every bridge across the Tuscarawas River in Stark County, except for one in Navarre, was swept away.

Floodwaters in Bolivar exceeded the previous record by four feet, though damage was minimized due to the fact that much of the town was on high ground. The Sad Iron Works, a plant at the Dover Manufacturing Company, and the Wagner Brothers Machine Shop, all located along the canal towpath just below the Factory Street Bridge in Canal Dover, collapsed due to floodwaters. Every bridge across the Tuscarawas and

Muskingum Rivers in Tuscarawas, Coshocton, and Muskingum Counties was destroyed by rain, which undermined the abutments.

Residents in New Philadelphia, on the south side of Lockport near Lock 13, were completely cut off from the surrounding countryside for days. Provisions had to be boated in. The residents of Port Washington and Newcomerstown were also isolated from the surrounding countryside for several days, and the canal channel through those towns was nearly obliterated. In Coshocton, floodwaters spread across 30 city blocks— 8 feet deep in some areas. In Zanesville, at the mouth of the Muskingum Improvement, the river crested at 51.8 feet, the highest stage ever recorded to that time, putting nearly 3,500 buildings under water.[8]

The northern part of the canal, north of the Portage Summit, wasn't hit quite as hard as other areas, but its citizens reacted a little more violently. Over the years, a number of fine homes and vacation areas had sprung up along the shores of the Ohio Canal Reservoirs, known by then as Portage Lakes. Nervous homeowners demanded that floodwaters be sent down the canal, away from their homes. Somehow, the banks of the reservoir were breached, sending thousands of tons of water cascading down the Tuscarawas and Muskingum Valleys. Rumors quickly spread that Summit County residents had dynamited a dam to relieve flooding of their homes. The Massillon City Council later investigated the alleged dynamiting of the Cottage Grove Dam near Paddy Ryan's Inn on a feeder from Turkeyfoot Lake to the canal and river. Summit County officials denied there was any dynamiting of dams or retaining walls to save cottages. The blame was placed on the excessive pressure of floodwaters on the earthen embankments of the dam. Whatever the cause, the embankment was breached around midnight on Sunday. The level of Turkeyfoot Lake dropped some six feet, with a subsequent drastic rise in the Tuscarawas River to the south and the Ohio Canal through Akron to the north.[9]

The closed gates on each of the 15 locks within the city of Akron became small dams, building up a head of water as high as eight feet above the gates. There were bypass channels around each lock, but the sudden increase in the volume of water from the Portage Lakes was too much. The crowds of people panicked and demanded the lock gates be dynamited. The gates of several locks within the city were dynamited, beginning with those at Lock 1 at Exchange Street on Monday night and including Lock 8, just south of Market Street around noon on Tuesday.

This uncoordinated dynamiting probably did little more than destroy the lock gates, damage some nearby buildings, and hasten the flood of water down the valley. Local papers questioned who had authorized the destruction of state property. Years later, stories were told about the flood, and John Henry Vance, an engineer at the B. F. Goodrich plant, "took credit" for supervising the destruction of Lock 1, a Mr. Madden for Lock 8 plus the nearby Alexander Building, and the city police for Lock 9.[10]

When the pent up water from the reservoir feeders and the pools behind the Akron locks were unleashed, they tore through the valley, shoving buildings from their foundations and destroying the canal channel from Akron to Peninsula. At Boston, local residents used 200 pounds of dynamite to blow up the mill dam in the Cuyahoga, hoping to relieve flooding in their town and sending torrents of water down the valley, destroying property and life along its banks.[11]

Along the Cleveland flats, at the junction of the Cuyahoga River and Lake Erie, devastation was tremendous, with docks, lumberyards, and businesses all having been swept away. Fourteen miles south of Cleveland, a state boat had been tied up at its usual slip near Stone Road, just south of Cleveland, over the Easter holiday. It was customary for an acting captain and the newest member of the crew, in this case 13-year-old Dillow Robinson, stepson of the actual captain, to be responsible for the craft and operations during the winter months. As soon as it became apparent that the amount of rainfall was going to be a problem, the captain and Robinson untied the craft and took it upstream to an iron bridge that carried Hillside Road over the canal. Their plan was to run the boat under the bridge for protection, lash it down, and then take the team and themselves to a nearby farmhouse on high ground to wait out the storm.

In an interview nearly 60 years later, Robinson related the difficulty the two men encountered in pushing the bow stem of the craft under the bridge in the rapidly rising canal waters. They finally gave up on this plan, lashed the boat as firmly as they could to the lee side of the bridge and to a couple of sturdy trees alongside the canal, and then quickly ran for cover. Their first refuge was with a family named Knapp who had a farm on higher ground near the canal. There were seven or eight people there. One man, named Murphy, who was the feeder tender at the nearby Pinery Feeder, kept going outside to look at the canal. During one of these excursions, he saw the iron bridge rise up, make a quarter turn, and sink into the canal, fortunately, shearing the lines that had attached the boat to it. He could see through the driving rain that the boat was still riding free. The worry was, however, that the boat would rest on the bridge, once the waters receded, and be impossible to get off without considerable damage.

Rising waters soon forced the group from the Knapp house to a farmhouse on top of a hill on Frase Road. When the captain and Robinson finally reached the boat several days later, they were greatly relieved to find it was not resting on the bridge but was riding peacefully in the rapidly receding water. The two men released the lines to the trees, got on board and, while the captain steered, allowed the craft to drift down to the slip at Stone Road, as Robinson put it, "right back where we was when we started."[12]

The statewide extent of death and destruction due to the Flood of 1913 exceeds all other weather events in Ohio's history, justifying the title "Ohio's greatest weather disaster." Rainfall over the state totaled 6 to 11 inches, and no part of the state was unaffected. The total death count was 467 and more than 40,000 homes were damaged or destroyed. The total cost of property damage totaled more than $100 million.[13]

Homes, businesses, and institutions across the state were destroyed by the flood, but the state's transportation system was also severely damaged. With nearly every river bridge destroyed, trains swept off tracks, railroad yards destroyed, and railroad lines torn up by the rampaging waters, it was months before the railroads and highways were back to any semblance of their former efficiency. The Ohio Canal had also suffered, but there was never an attempt to repair it for boat operation. Regular boating had ceased on the Ohio & Erie Canal in 1905 or 1906. The Flood of 1913, by washing away many of the canal's feeder dams and seriously damaging banks throughout the state, had put an end to the canal as a viable, through transportation system.[14]

AFTER THE FLOOD, 1913–1929

Much of the economic reasoning behind the attempted rebuild of the canal in the early 1900s was based on the long-term waterpower leases the state had made with numerous private commercial interests. Many of these were lucrative and still in effect after the flood. Therefore, when a good supply of water could be obtained with little effort or expense, the state made that repair to keep the waterpower leases intact.

The American Steel Wire Mill, located along the berm side of the canal between Five Mile and Eight Mile Locks in Cleveland, was a big water customer of the state. The Pinery Feeder Dam at Brecksville had not been damaged by the flood. There were a few breaks in the banks on the feeder level, but state forces quickly repaired that stretch of canal for hydraulic power and cooling water transmission. By the end of the year, some minor repairs had been made to various sections, and the supervisor of Public Works report for 1913 stated the condition of the Ohio Canal in stark terms:

> The flood of 1913 wrought considerable damage to the Ohio & Erie Canal. At the present time, water is maintained in the canal as follows; From Brecksville to Cleveland, a distance of seventeen miles, a good head of water. From Lock No. 12 in the City of Akron to Brecksville the canal is practically destroyed. The distance is 16 miles. There are several breaks in the banks, especially at Peninsula and Boston. The Summit Level from Lock No. 1 to Massillon, a distance of 21 miles, has a supply of water. From below Massillon to Zoar Dam, a distance of 18 miles, there is no water. This stretch passes through the towns of Navarre and Bolivar. There is a good feed of water from Zoar Dam to Sugar Creek, a mile below Canal Dover, a distance of eleven miles. From the latter point to Roscoe Aqueduct, a distance of 42 miles, no water. Six Mile Dam to Dresden, a distance of 24 miles, a fair supply of water.[15]

The Portage Summit level of the Ohio Canal, due to the Portage Lakes reservoirs, provided a good supply of water after the flood, and that 10-mile stretch of canal was ready to supply hydraulic power and cooling water to a number of industries in south Akron and Barberton. The state even placed a satellite office at the head of that waterway, Lock 1 at Exchange Street, for administrative and maintenance purposes. The excess water leaving that stretch of canal north of Lock 1 was allowed to flow through town in a hastily repaired canal channel through the ruined locks of Akron and into the Little Cuyahoga River below Lock 15. This resulted in a great deal of flooding and sewage control problems that had to be dealt with later.

The stretch of canal in Stark County through Canal Fulton and Massillon was fed through a seven-mile channel from a large swamp in Summit

County. This source was still intact after the 1913 flood, and with a few repairs to the banks of the canal and feeder, that stretch was able to provide hydraulic power and cooling water to industries in Massillon.[16]

The Six Mile Dam across the Walhonding River above Coshocton had been rebuilt in 1907–09 primarily to ensure a good supply of water to what would become the Ohio Light and Heating Company in 1910. By 1912 the company had constructed and was operating a new electricity-generating plant along the Walhonding Branch Canal about a quarter of a mile above Roscoe. That dam was not damaged in the 1913 flood, and the plant soon resumed providing electrical power for the city of Coshocton.[17]

The rest of the Ohio Canal between Cleveland and Dresden was mostly ignored by the state and legislature. However, they did not abandon the canal but kept it officially open for many years for hydraulic purposes. The floodwaters had scarcely receded before there was talk, primarily around Cleveland, of building a modern ship canal from Cleveland and Lake Erie to the Muskingum River at Dresden. A heated debate sprung up along the route of the proposed canal. While the debate raged and afterward, the state hung on to the canal's right-of-way. This led to some building restrictions in certain parts of Massillon and Akron throughout the rest of the first three decades of the twentieth century.

The state owned a narrow strip of land running directly through Massillon and Akron. Rather than have a 60-foot swath of water and embankments divide the towns, city officials obtained renewable, 15-year leases from the state at so much per square foot of water/embankment. The water in the canal had to be maintained to serve industries downstream, but the city officials of Massillon and Akron were free to erect buildings across the canal. The first floors of buildings were supported by heavy steel beams laid across sturdy piers sunk into the canal bed. Boiler rooms for heating were installed in deep excavations beneath the towpath. The original McClain Grocery warehouse in Massillon was erected along the canal's berm bank north of Tremont Street in 1889. When an addition was made, it was constructed over the canal right-of-way. Two great culverts in the building's first floor north and south walls carried the canal beneath the structure.[18]

Many Massillon businesses along North and South Main Street or the west side of South Erie Avenue had the canal in either their backyards or basements. One such business was the Massillon Auto Sales and Storage

Company, located on the first floor of a building constructed over the canal along South Erie Street. The summer humidity in that showroom, scant inches above water of the canal flowing through a channel below the first floor, played hob with the nickel plating on the autos. The showroom didn't last long. In Akron's case, the waterway through town was the tail race of the hydraulic channel from Lock 1 at Exchange Street south to the Little Cuyahoga River at Lock 15. Unlike in Massillon, there were few restrictions on the width and depth of the channel. However, there had to be sufficient volume to carry any surge in the race due to heavy rains.

According to local history, the Civic Movie Theater on South Main Street was built in 1923 over the canal waterway in the vicinity of Lock 4. Many theater patrons claimed to hear the rushing water beneath their feet when the rains had been particularly heavy. When the M. McNeil Department store management wanted to build a parking deck addition to its downtown Akron store in the late 1920s, it was built over the canal and Lock 3. The first level of the parking deck was built on pillars over the canal, giving scant headroom over the years for anyone wishing to see Lock 3. It also afforded the only lock on the Ohio & Erie Canal with a roof. Farther down the canal, south of Bowery Street, five store rooms were constructed on "stilts" over the flowing canal channel and Locks 7 and 8 south of Market Street. Between Market and North Streets, the canal was again in open country for a few blocks as it cascaded down the precipitous slope that contained Locks 9 through 14 before entering the Little Cuyahoga River just below Lock 15.[19]

Dillow Robinson stayed on the state boat in Pinery Narrows until 1917, working for the state primarily maintaining the waterway for hydraulic and cooling water for the Wire Company. The state boat had only four or five men in the crew, and perennial flooding in spring and fall continued to wreak havoc with the canal banks. Now, though, scarcely would the rains cease when a large crew of steelworkers from the mill would descend on the channel to help make it watertight. Robinson left the canal to open a grocery with his stepfather. He then joined the army in 1918 and fought in France during World War 1. Upon mustering out, he tried a variety of jobs, ending up on the canal maintenance gang in 1921 for a two-year stint. During his hiatus, the wooden state boat had disappeared, and the new method of conveyance along the canal was a Model T Ford truck.[20]

Johnny Moore, the supervisor of the state boat in the section between

Canal Fulton and Massillon had only one helper, but he maintained that section of the canal steadily for many years. In fact, through the judicious help of high school boys during the summer months and during the school closings in 1918 due to the flu epidemic, Johnny was able to repair the banks and open the canal for hydraulic purposes, as far south as Navarre by the summer of 1918.[21]

Throughout the 1910s and early 1920s, the local municipalities—Akron, Canal Fulton, Massillon, and Navarre—through which the canal still ran were forced to build over or around the strip of canal land running through their towns. Over the years, however, any notion of a lake-to-river ship canal shifted emphasis from the Akron-Massillon route to one farther east, along the Mahoning Valley through Youngstown's booming iron and steel area. A number of proposals for the state to officially abandon the Ohio Canal through the towns along the Cuyahoga and Tuscarawas were initiated and sent to the legislature. Finally, in July 1929, the state of Ohio officially abandoned the last section of the Ohio & Erie Canal for navigational purposes.[22] The Ohio & Erie Canal began with a legislative act in February 1825 and was abandoned by a legislative act in July 1929. Ohio's canal era had lasted just slightly more than 100 years.

Even though the Ohio & Erie Canal was abandoned as a transportation system, neither the waterway nor the state was quite through with the other. Significant stretches of canal in or near Cleveland, Akron, Barberton, Canal Fulton, Massillon, and Coshocton maintained water levels with hydraulic and cooling water potential. The state promptly began negotiating long-term leases for these and other canal properties. The city of Massillon, for example, signed a 99-year lease for the state's use of the strip of canal lands within the city boundaries. The lease went into effect in 1931 at an annual rental of $12,226.

The country was in a severe financial depression by then, and the few industries in the Massillon area requiring canal waterpower or cooling water quickly went bankrupt, along with many other businesses. City officials wanted to use the canal lands for business and manufacturing purposes. They attempted to get the canal filled within the city limits. An agreement was finally reached with the state in 1933 to defer the yearly lease payments and use them to pay off a loan to finance a large underground storm water system within the canal bed, finally burying the old canal beneath the streets and businesses of Massillon.[23]

During 1938, the Ohio Conservation Bureau of the Department of Public Works authorized $25,000 for use in the stretch of the abandoned Ohio & Erie Canal from Lake Street at the northern edge of Massillon north through Canal Fulton to the feeder near Lake Lucerne. With the money granted from the state, manpower from the federally sponsored Civilian Conservation Corps, and expertise and equipment from the Stark County Engineers, this five-mile stretch of the Ohio Canal was redeveloped into recreational lands for hiking, camping, fishing, and hunting.[24] The canal structures were refurbished and the feeder channel from Summit County tightened up. A small grove in the Millport area, which had been popular among Massillon picnickers traveling on the last canal boats, was spruced up, with an old iron bridge brought out of storage and placed over the canal for access between the towpath and the new motor highway, Erie Street. A constant head of water was maintained from the feeder to a new concrete dam erected across the canal channel just above Lake Street. The canal below was allowed to go dry. In a separate project, the state built a roadside park at the Fulton Lock that enlarged the recreational appeal of the area.[25] For many years, this stretch of the Ohio & Erie Canal provided a place of relaxation and enjoyment. Unfortunately no entity was initiated to maintain this parkland, and it eventually was allowed to deteriorate.[26]

Massillon's federal loan was paid off in 1947. In 1949, the city issued bonds to raise $125,000 (plus two years' worth of back rental caused by a disagreement over the current value of the land) to purchase 1.7 miles of the Ohio Canal through the heart of the city.[27]

The state office in Akron continued to handle disbursement of canal water rentals. A new canal office building was erected adjacent to Lock 1 at Exchange Street in Akron in 1948–49. This office continues to service between eight and ten customers annually.[28] Water leasing in this area became such a lucrative business for the state that additional reservoirs were built on the Portage Summit in 1936 and 1963. In 1951, the city of Akron initiated an extensive project along the Ohio Canal from Market Street to North Street. Concrete walls, sluices, and dams were constructed in and along the canal channel, and structures were built to augment the flow of storm waters through the valley.

Then, beginning in 1964 and continuing into 1967, the city of Akron rejuvenated a section of its downtown by deepening the channel of the canal and lining it with concrete from Bowery Street to about 100 feet north of Ash Street. This was then enclosed in a concrete box, about 20 feet by 16 feet, from Bowery to Market and covered over.[29]

Stark County commissioners obtained all the canal lands within their county from the state in 1964, thanks to the Navarre Village solicitor Ralph Regula and *Canton Repository* reporter Al Simpson. Largely due to Simpson's weekly column, local interest in the canal era was generated, resulting in the construction of a canal boat replica on the banks of the watered canal in Canal Fulton during 1967–70. The Stark County Park District, formed in 1968, began a steady project to preserve the canal lands within the county's borders. The Canal Fulton Heritage Society and the Stark County Historical Society joined forces in 1970 to build and launch the canal boat replica *St. Helena II.* Its successor still gives two-and-a-half-mile rides down the canal to Lock 4 and back during the summer months. In 1964, Edward Montgomery, an industrialist from Coshocton County, began restoring one canal-era building in Roscoe after the section of canal through that old town was supplanted by a highway. Now, the village of Roscoe and the city of Coshocton are known all over the state for their efforts in preserving a bit of Ohio's canal era. "Mad Marshall" Jacobs, a Coshocton native, built and launched a canal boat replica, the *Monticello II,* near Roscoe in 1971. Its successor, the *Monticello III,* now carries passengers during the summer months.

The lease of that stretch of canal from Brecksville (Pinery Feeder) to the Wire Mill (below Eight Mile Lock) was a lucrative and long-term lease that ran into the 1970s. About that time, however, a desire to protect Ohio's history and green spaces began to be expressed. In 1974, efforts within local park departments and a surge in federal interest culminated in the formation of the federally funded Cuyahoga Valley National Recreation Area. A large portion of the Wire Company's waterpower lease, no longer vital to production, was turned over to the fledgling park area. Portions of this lease were also obtained by the park departments of Cuyahoga and Summit Counties. Sections of the Ohio Canal towpath were converted into hiking and biking trails, and another generation became familiar with the term Ohio & Erie Canal. The CVNRA became the Cuyahoga Valley National Park in December 2000.

The city of Akron built a park around Lock 2 in 1984 and one around Lock 3 in 2000 and is laboriously uncovering more of the canal that the city covered up in the 1960s. In 1974, a private group, the Cascades Locks Park Organization, began working with the Metropolitan Park District for Akron and Summit County to refurbish the canal lands from Market to North Streets.

In 1996, the federally mandated Ohio & Erie Canal Heritage Corridor was designated between Lake Erie at Cleveland in Cuyahoga County and Zoar (later extended to New Philadelphia) in Tuscarawas County. A park district was formed within Tuscarawas County in 2002 to work with similar districts in Cuyahoga, Summit, and Stark on the Ohio & Erie Canal Heritage Corridor project. Together, county, state, and federal entities, along with the private sector where possible, are redeveloping what remains of Ohio & Erie Canal lands into recreational areas. The Akron State Canal office now works as a partner with local park entities, leasing the canal lands to them and providing maintenance for the watered canal system between Akron and Barberton. This office maintains a fleet of watercraft, including one weed harvester, three barges, and two power boats, to provide this service.[30]

Just prior to the turn of the last century, an interurban line used a portion of the canal towpath in the Licking Narrows east of Newark. In 1938, the Works Progress Administration turned the canal towpath/interurban route into a gravel road. Two high points of that road included a tunnel for the trolley line and a twin-arch stone culvert for the canal. Construction of Dillon Dam in the 1950s and 1960s rerouted the railroad and closed that road, but some of the canal artifacts and the tunnel can still be seen in the Black Hand Gorge State Nature Preserve, which was designated as such in 1975.[31]

A small park, adjacent to Route 79 near Heath, Ohio, in Licking County incorporates the remnants of Lock 1, where the opening ceremonies to the Ohio Canal took place on July 4, 1825. Four locks at Lockville are maintained by the Fairfield County Historical Parks District. Picnic areas and hiking trails are maintained as well as signage that informs Ohioans of their canal-era heritage. In 2006, the remnants of the only lock in Lockville were incorporated into the town's Blacklick Park. The Pickaway County Park District, formed in January 2002, includes an eight-mile stretch of the Ohio Canal running along Canal Road south of Circleville. The southern end of this area includes a plot that the WPA converted into a small park in the 1930s. Another small park in Waverly, located in Pike County at the southern edge of the town along Route 23, includes remnants of Lock 44. Ohio's White Lake in Pike County contains portions of Ohio Canal lands. The lake, built during the 1930s by the WPA, was dedicated as a state park in 1949.[32]

Today, large portions of the Ohio Canal are gone. Through the efforts of many individuals and organizations, however, bits of the canal's structure and the history of Ohio during the canal era will live on. Ideally, future generations of Ohioans will look up from their recreational pursuits along the valleys of the Cuyahoga, Muskingum, Licking, and Scioto Rivers and occasionally remember and thank Governor Brown, Alfred Kelley, Micajaw Williams, or the many burly boatmen whose spirits no doubt still frequent these valleys.

New outlet (1878) Lock 42 from the canal into Cuyahoga River at Cleveland.

Schuster Brewery at Millport, Stark County. Note the sturdy, blunt-nosed canal boat used to carry barrels of beer 4½ miles south to the bottling plant in Massillon. (Courtesy of the Massillon Museum)

McLaughlin dry dock in Canal Fulton, Stark County. (Drawing by Waldo Streby)

The *Sassykanudrop*, a "party boat," near Canal Dover, Tuscarawas County.

The state boat *Dick Goram* in Fairfield County.

Repairing the Walhonding Aqueduct, Coshocton County.

State dredge in Massillon, Stark County.

The canal dredge bunk boat, *Katherine,* and her happy crew.

Daily Brother's Construction Company rebuilding Trenton feeder dam in Tuscarawas County in 1907. (Courtesy of the Daily family)

J. N. Krissner Company rebuilding Lock 15 in Trenton, Tuscarawas County, in 1907.

Lock 15 after Sept. 1911 flood, looking up the canal, Tuscarawas (Trenton) Village.

Lock 8 in Akron during 1913 flood. (Courtesy of Ted Dettling)

Lock 17 at flood, Village of Seventeen, Tuscarawas County.

Ohio & Erie Canal dry in Navarre, Ohio.

Locks 26 and 27, Roscoe, Coshocton County. (Courtesy of Louis Baus and Roscoe Village Foundation Photo files)

Houseboat in Stark County after canal was abandoned. (Courtesy of Canal Fulton Heritage Society)

⚒ 6 ⚒
Effects of the Canal

THE BENEFITS

Many people believe that Ohio's canal system made the state what it is today. Due to the relative ease the canals made of transporting goods between the interior of Ohio and eastern markets, business, industry, population, and money flowed into the state. The canals provided the money and the impetus for the state's citizens and the country's entrepreneurs to invest in railroads during the 1850s and 1860s.

The canals provided both direct and indirect benefits to the state. The direct benefits included net revenues from tolls, waterpower sales, and rental of canal lands, all of which paid for the maintenance and operation of the canals, with a surplus of a little over $5 million. However, this income did not cover the construction and interest on the loans for the canals.[1] Some argue that it would have been smarter and cheaper to have waited until "it was time to railroad" and then build railroads.

The canals of Ohio were not constructed to make money. They were constructed so the state could survive economically. While they did provide the needed cheap, reliable transportation, they also lead to other important benefits for Ohio—increased property values, an influx of population, and the development of the state's agricultural, industrial, and political climate.

It is difficult, if not impossible, to imagine what life was like in the new state of Ohio prior to the mid-1820s. The soil was rich and, it was suspected, the natural resources of the country were prolific and easily obtainable.

In 1810, the population of Ohio was 230,760, making Ohio the thirteenth most populous state in the nation. After the War of 1812, immigrants from the eastern United States and from foreign shores poured into this new state. By 1820, only 10 years later, the population had more than doubled to 581,434, making Ohio the country's fifth most populous state.

The bulk of this population was clustered by necessity near the banks of the navigable rivers. The natural rivers of Ohio were nearly the only transportation routes into and out of the state. Prior to the opening of the Ohio & Erie Canal, the economic progress of Ohio was stagnant. The cost of transporting goods over the Allegheny Mountain Range to the eastern markets of New York, Baltimore, and Philadelphia removed any prospect of profit from such endeavors. The only market open to the majority of Ohioans was New Orleans, at best a sporadic and unpredictable one but also a politically inappropriate market to cultivate, as it did not promote ties between the old East and the new West.[2]

With the population of the state growing rapidly in the 1820s, Ohioans needed a transportation system to the eastern markets immediately, not at some unspecified time in the future. It is doubtful that anyone in Ohio in the 1820s recommended waiting for the railroads. The directors of the fledgling Baltimore & Ohio Railroad "lucked out" when they initiated that road in 1825, but the truth is that even those directors saw the rail line as more of a horse-drawn public carrier than as a formal transportation company. It wasn't until the mid-1830s, a full decade after the initiation of Ohio's canals, that certain improvements in the design of steam locomotives made them viable for light American iron rails. Even then, it took another 20 years before railroads were economically competitive to canals in Ohio.[3]

Primarily due to the lack of readily accessible markets, only one-sixth of Ohio had been cleared and cultivated by the early 1820s. The northwestern section of the state was in fact a wilderness—Native American tribes still lived there—and the rest of the state could hardly be called settled. Yet by 1850, mainly due to Ohio canals, the state population had climbed to the third highest in the nation with a total of 1,987,329 residents. Even more important was the fact that though Ohio was relatively strong in industrial activity in 1820, little of that activity was of an exportable nature. By 1850, Ohio ranked third in exporting manufactured and mineral products to the rest of the nation and beyond.[4]

Construction of Ohio's canals began in 1825. In just 20 years, the canals, along with the hard work and entrepreneurial ingenuity of Ohio's citizens, pulled the state out of the economic depths of the 1820s and thrust it into a position of power and influence in the nation. The effects of canal construction were felt immediately. Canal contractors were paid in cash, and they paid their workers the same. Perhaps for the first time in Ohio's history, cash money was in circulation.

The tangible effects of the Ohio Canal were felt immediately after the opening of the first short section to Lake Erie on July 4, 1827. The first beneficiaries were northeastern Ohio farmers who were able to profitably grow wheat for the first time. Before the canal was operational, the price of wheat near what later became Akron could be sold for only 20 to 30 cents per bushel. But by 1833, the first full year of operation for the through canal from lake to river, it could easily be sold for 75 cents to a dollar per bushel.[5] It is no wonder that many Ohioans, tasting prosperity for the first time, called this waterway Ohio's Grand Canal.

Wheat prices in eastern Ohio between 1826 and 1858 rose on average from 25 cents to $1.08 a bushel, while corn went from 25 cents to 70 cents per bushel. Meanwhile, imported sugar dropped from 9 to 7 cents a pound, while coffee fell from 15 to 12 cents. Property values in the 37 canal counties in Ohio increased 14 times between 1826 and 1859.[6]

The 12 counties along the main route of the Ohio Canal did even better. New towns sprang up in the counties with newly constructed canals. Akron and Massillon grew to be industry and population leaders in the state. Akron, founded in 1825, reached a population of 3,206 by 1850. Massillon, founded a year later in 1826, had an estimated population of more than 1,000 by 1836. The town of Cleveland, with a population of only 606 in 1820 (after nearly three decades of existence), exploded from a population of 1,076 in 1830 to 6,071 just a decade later.[7]

Mineral coal was mined and shipped profitably on the canal, first near the Portage Summit of the Ohio Canal and later south along the Ohio and Hocking Canals. Fledgling industries sprung up along the canal using the natural waterpower adjacent to the locks at a time when steam power was almost too costly and underdeveloped for profitable use. The towns of Cleveland, Akron, and Massillon on the Ohio Canal and Youngstown on the Pennsylvania & Ohio Canal branch parlayed the fast starts given them by the canals and, with a lot of help from the railroads, became by the end of the nineteenth century four of the most prosperous industrial centers in northeast Ohio. The towns of Canal Dover, Newark, Columbus, and Portsmouth also were given jump starts by the Ohio Canal.

In addition to developing the state commercially, the canals also assisted in the state's political development. The agitation for the canal project, the fight in the legislature, the celebration in the passage of the Canal Act, and Governor Clinton's tour of the state aroused the people and welded them into an acting political power with seemingly endless vigor. Just as the Erie Canal made New York the "Empire State" and Pennsylvania's canals made Pennsylvania the second state in the union, the Ohio Canal system made Ohio the third most prominent and influential state in the union.[8]

It is interesting to consider the Ohio Canal as an economic extension of and feeder to New York's Erie Canal. Without the Erie Canal, which provided communication between Lake Erie and the New York City market via the Hudson River, a canal through Ohio would have had little economic impact on the citizenry. That is undoubtedly why the early canal advocates in each state supported the efforts of the other. It is also why, for many of the early freight and passenger lines, end points of the two canals were often blurred.[9]

But New York's political leaders were perhaps more astute about transportation competition within their state than were their counterparts in Ohio. In any event, the political climate in Ohio during the 1850s made it impossible for the canal system to be improved and to compete with railroads (unlike in New York where improvements were made). That foresight may also explain why the Erie Canal still operates today, drawing millions of tourist dollars to New York, while that is not the case in Ohio.

Still, the Ohio Canal was instrumental in providing the initial impetus to many of the towns and cities in eastern and central Ohio. And while a number of towns used the canal to leap to industrial prominence, some, such as Peninsula, Canal Fulton, and Roscoe, made the initial jump to prosperity but withered and limped along as the water in the canals dried up. Ironically, several towns that maintained their canals, or a semblance of them, are now experiencing a new prosperity as canal tourist areas.[10] Despite the overall financial loss of the canals, it is fairly apparent that the present state of Ohio would be drastically different had the canals not been built when they were.

Life on the Canal

As much as the locks, aqueducts, channels, and boats of the Ohio Canal may hold a fascination for us today, it is the people of the canal era, particularly those who lived and worked on and along the Ohio Canal, who made the canal history we appreciate today.

When the Ohio Canal was new, the boatmen and the people who worked on and lived along it were at the forefront of everyday life. They came from the ranks of the common man and the well-to-do entrepreneur. They were a combination of early nineteenth-century Ohioans, perhaps with a bit more of an adventurous spirit than others. They enjoyed the continuous movement and the hustle and bustle of life on the canal.

During the 1820s and 1830s, the Ohio Canal was considered to be the economic saving of Ohio. As a result, the canal channel itself, which ran through the business heart of every town along its route, was highly regarded. In fact, many towns were founded and grew prosperous because of their intimacy with the Ohio Canal. Stately homes were built with the canal literally in their front yards.[11] Though the average boatman was always thought of as part of the working class, captains of line boats during the 1830s and 1840s were considered part of the elite class of town and were esteemed by ordinary citizens and envied by young boys.

The canal boatman, by the very nature of his constant movement, skill, and willingness to use his fists when arguments arose, became a bit of a folk hero in early Ohio. What the cowboy was to the youth of the mid-twentieth century, the boatman was, perhaps, to the Ohio youth of the mid-nineteenth century.

However, as the Ohio Canal became less important in the lives of everyday citizens and the railroad became more important, the status of a canal boatman slowly slipped away. Home sites along the canal were no longer so desirable, and names of canal areas began to reflect their changed ethnicity, such as "Italy Hill" below Lock 6 in Navarre and "Black Dog Crossing" above Lock 19 near Akron.[12]

Through the 1840s, most boatmen worked for a company, a freight, and passenger line. Their lives were much like those of today's long-distance truckers. They would be away from their families during the summer for days and weeks at a time. Then, in the winter, they would be at home for weeks or months, when they might repair equipment, do seasonal farm work, or work at a nearby factory. After the railroads provided stiffer competition to the freight and passenger lines, more independent haulers came onto the canals. These were men who owned, or were buying, their own boat. Most of them carried their families onboard, living in the stern cabin of the three-cabin freighter.[13]

Boatmen and their families separated from and drifted out of the mainstream. While the more conventional citizens may have still envied them slightly, the boatmen were generally frowned upon and considered outsiders. They became a close-knit group and developed a slang, almost a language, of their own. Daughters of boatmen married sons of boatmen, and daughters of farmers along the canal married sons of boatmen. A clannish group, many canal families were related to each other, and entire generations grew up on the canal and became isolated from the mainstream.[14] Boatmen knew their lives were different from those of a "Town Jake," and they relished that difference. They were always on the move, albeit at less than two miles an hour, while the Town Jake was anchored to his land, never traveling more than a few miles from his birthplace his entire life.[15]

Boatmen were a happy people, proud of their heritage, which they preserved in story and song, and apparently impervious to what the future might bring. As the Ohio Canal physically deteriorated during the late-nineteenth century, the ranks of the boatmen thinned, but the ones remaining made up for their diminished numbers with their zeal for canal life. By the turn of the century, an estimated 100 families, each with a boat, still made their living on the foreshortened Ohio Canal.[16]

Many of these families were still on the canal in 1906 when the northern division was shut down temporarily for the rebuild. Boatmen stored their craft in any widewater that was available. Akron's Lower Basin, convenient to Perkins school and the nearby Goodrich Rubber Plant, became a veritable floating city as boatmen converted their craft into temporary quarters with wooden lath and tar paper. Many of the homes were still there as late as 1929, when the state officially abandoned the Ohio & Erie Canal.[17]

Eventually, the vast majority of the remaining boatmen left the canal for other work on railroads, farms, and mines. A few couldn't adjust to town life and literally wandered the country looking for something that no longer existed. As individual boatmen grew older, they became fodder for reporters, with stories abounding in local papers about the last canal boatman. In general, they regretted the passing of canal life and wished they could make one more trip on the "raging canal" before they died.[18] During the 1960s, 1970s, and 1980s, the remaining boatmen in northeastern Ohio (all of whom had been children when they worked the canal) and a few people who lived along the canal when it was operational were interviewed on tape by such canal historians as Dave Lieberth, Terry Woods, Nancy Lonsinger, and Edith McNally. Thanks to them and several more like them, the memories and words of the boatmen can still tell us a bit about life on and along the Ohio & Erie Canal.

Appendix

Rebuild Contracts of the Ohio & Erie Canal

From the 1909 Board of Public Works Report

Description	Contractor	Date	Cost
Dredging Akron to Cleveland	D.E. Sullivan & Son	10/10/1905	$79,741.64
Weigh Lock at Cleveland	State Forces	05/28/1906	583.64
Cuyahoga River Bulkhead*	Standard Cont. Co.	06/25/08	30,000.00
Cuyahoga River Bulkhead	Standard Cont. Co.	01/09/06	5,148.66
Waste between Locks 41 and 42	State Forces		467.19
Lock 41N	Carmichael & Co.	02/14/05	11,929.37
Sluice between Locks 40 and 41N	Carmichael & Co.	02/14/05	711.10
Stone protection Cuyahoga River	State Forces		467.52
Sluice between Locks 40 and 41N	Carmichael & Co.	02/14/05	717.06
Sluice between Locks 40 and 41N	Carmichael & Co.	02/14/05	664.88
Culvert between Locks 40 and 41N	Carmichael & Co.	02/14/05	1,177.82
Sluice between Locks 40 and 41N	Carmichael & Co.	02/14/05	559.24
Lock 40N	Carmichael & Co.	02/14/05	4,061.41

Description	Contractor	Date	Cost
Mill Creek Aqueduct**	Carmichael & Co.	02/14/05	3,581.71
Culvert between Locks 30 and 40N	Carmichael & Co.	02/14/05	772.69
Culvert between Locks 39 and 40N	Com'rs Cuyahoga Co.	1909	718.42
Culvert between Locks 39 and 40N	Com'rs Cuyahoga Co.	1909	718.42
Lock 39N	Carmichael & Co.	02/14/05	4,619.32
Sluice between Locks 38 and 39N	Carmichael & Co.	02/14/05	702.17
Culvert between Locks 38 and 39N	Carmichael & Co.	02/14/05	1,387.07
Wasteway between Locks 38 and 39N	State forces		694.95
Culvert between Locks 38 and 39N	Com'rs Cuyahoga Co.	1909	694.95
Culvert between Locks 38 and 39N	Com'rs Cuyahoga Co.	1909	718.34
Lock 39N	Carmichael & Co.	02/14/05	4,734.93
Tinker's Creek Aqueduct**	Carmichael & Co.	02/14/05	4,535.94
Sluice between Locks 37 and 38N	Carmichael & Co.	02/14/05	582.55
Lock 37N	Carmichael & Co.	02/14/05	4,300.22
Sluice between Locks 36 and 37N	Carmichael & Co.	02/14/05	514.73
Sluice between Locks 36 and 37N	Carmichael & Co.	02/14/05	663.11
Sluice between Locks 36 and 37N	Carmichael & Co.	02/14/05	529.73
Sluice between Locks 36 and 37N	Carmichael & Co.	02/14/05	481.37
Mud catcher at Galley Run	State forces	1908	1,984.86
Sluice and Weir Brecksville Feeder	State forces	1905	2,015.62
Head gates Brecksville feeder	State forces	1905	1,096.19
Dam at Brecksville	State forces	1905	266.69

DESCRIPTION	CONTRACTOR	DATE	COST
Lock 36N	Carmichael & Co.	02/14/05	4,487.06
High water waste way	State forces	1906	151.40
Lock 35N	P.T. McCourt	02/14/05	5,334.98
Sluice between Locks 34 and 35N	P.T. McCourt	02/14/05	701.52
High water waste way	State forces	1906	151.40
Lock 34N	P.T. McCourt	02/14/06	5,632.73
Lock 33N	P.T. McCourt	02/14/05	4,893.73
Culvert between Locks 32 and 33N	State forces	1906	60.00
Lock 32N	P.T. McCourt	02/14/05	5,045.85
Lock 31N	P.T. McCourt	02/14/05	6,161.05
Lock 31N	State forces	1908	2,917.44
Sluice between Locks 30 and 31N	P. T. McCourt	02/14/05	600.49
Head gates Peninsula Feeder	State forces	1905	1,117.38
Dam at Peninsula	State forces	1905	1,348.48
Lock 30N	P.T. McCourt	02/14/05	5,798.79
Lock 29N	P.T. McCourt (Ely)	02/14/05	8,178.69
Peninsula Aqueduct**	P.T. McCourt	02/14/05	12,171.51
Lock 28N	P.T. McCourt	02/14/05	5,334.95
Lock 27N	McGerry & McGowan	02/14/05	5,938.42
Sluice between Locks 26 and 27N	McGarry & McGowan	02/14/05	395.93
Lock 26N	McGarry & McGowan	02/14/05	4,914.87
Sluice between Locks 25 and 26N	McGarry & McGowan	02/14/05	523.51
Ira Culvert between Locks 25 and 26N	McGarry & McGowan	02/14/05	4,288.00
Lock 25N	McGarry & McGowan	02/14/05	5,862.39
Lock 24N	McGarry & McGowan	02/14/05	5,864.83
Sluice between Locks 23 and 24N	McGarry & McGowan	02/14/05	407.49
Sluice between Locks 23 and 24N	McGarry & McGowan	02/14/05	473.53

Description	Contractor	Date	Cost
Sand Run Aqueduct	McGarry & McGowan	02/14/05	2,127.70
Sluice between Locks 23 and 24N	McGarry & McGowan	02/14/05	631.95
Sluice between Locks 23 and 24N	McGarry & McGowan	02/14/05	628.00
Culvert between Locks 23 and 24N	State forces	1905	372.74
Lock 23N	McGarry & McGowan	02/14/05	5,323.26
Lock 22N	McGarry & McGowan	02/14/05	4,813.23
Sluice between Locks 21 and 22N	Wise and Ely	09/08/08	944.54
Sluice between Locks 21 and 22N	Wise & Ely	09/08/08	1,036.24
Dam, Little Cuyahoga River	A.A. Likens	08/13.07	2,138.84
Lock 21N	McGarry & McGowan	08/01/06	5,142.95
Lock 20N	McGarry & McGowan	08/01/06	4,914.48
Lock 19N	McGarry & McGowan	08/01/06	5,828.90
Lock 18N	McGarry & McGowan	08/01/06	5,608.97
Lock 17N	McGarry & McGowan	08/01/06	5,138.78
Sluice between Locks 16 and 17N	Wise & Ely	09/08/06	890.58
Lock 16N	McGarry & McGowan	08/01/06	6,314.70
Lock 15N	McGarry & McGowan	08/01/06	5,502.61
Lock 14N	S.W. Parshall	08/01/06	5,236.35
Lock 13N	S.W. Parshall	08/01/06	5,730.03
Lock 12N	S.W. Parshall	08/01/06	5,453.46
Lock 11N	S.W. Parshall	08/01/06	5,406.28
Lock 10N	S.W. Parshall	08/01/06	6,466.84
Sluice around Lock 10N	Reed, Deeds & Son	08/17//07	430.06
Lock 9N	S.W. Parshall	08/01/06	5,692.41
Lock 8N	S.W. Parshall	08/01/06	5,305.75
Sluice around Lock 8N	State forces	1906	2,173.48
Lock 7N	P.T. McCourt	08/01/06	6,520.96
Sluice between Locks 7 and 8N	Wise & Ely	09/08/08	590.99

Description	Contractor	Date	Cost
Lock 6N	P.T. McCourt	08/01/06	6,140.72
Lock 5N	P.T. McCourt	08/01/06	6,987.00
Lock 4N	P.T. McCourt	08/01/06	7,246.46
Lock 3N	P.T. McCourt	08/01/06	5,400.64
Lock 2N	P.T. McCourt	08/01/06	5,633.35
Lock 1N	P.T. McCourt	08/01/06	5,432.46
Retaining wall at Lock 1N	P.T. McCourt	08/01/06	1,176.16
Dam, Tuscarawas Feeder	Kinnear Bros.	06/08/08	2,090.22
New Reservoir Summit County	Franklin Brothers	08/13/07	29,772.64
Waste way Summit level	James Wildes	03/13/07	672.60
Culvert at Mud Run	James McGowan	08/28/06	3,183.74
Dredging Portage Summit	State forces	1909	3,510.46
Bank protection Portage Summit	J.W. Bennage	09/1909	3,510.46
Lock 1S	James Wildes	03/13/07	4,684.49
Dredging Barberton, Canal Fulton	Paul & Henry	05/11/09	1,975.21
Wolf Creek Aqueduct***	Burns & Engle	03/13/07	13,839.31
Lock 2S	S.W. Parshall	03/13/07	6,215.33
Lock No. 3S	James Wildes	03/13/07	4,996.61
Clinton Guard Lock and Sluice S	James Wildes	03/13/07	3,493.51
Sluice between Locks 3 and 4S	James Wildes	03/13/1907	578.72
Culvert repaired between Locks3 and 4	State forces	1907	186.31
Sluice between Locks 3 and 4S	James Wildes	03/13/1907	578.72
Waste way between Locks 3 and 4S	Fauver & Renich	03/13/1907	736.11
Waste way between Locks 3 and 4S	James Wildes	03/13/1907	833.19

Description	Contractor	Date	Cost
Lock 4 S	Fauver & Renich	03/13/1907	4,832.25
Culvert between Locks 4 and 5S	State Forces	1907	653.26
Sluice between Locks 4 and 5S	Fauver & Renich	03/13/1907	660.32
Sluice between Locks 4 and 5S	Fauver & Rencih	03/13/1907	571.94
Waste way and sluice, Massillon	T.H. Watson & Son	05/11/1909	1,048.95
Lock 5S (repair)	W.H. Vogt & Son	06/23/1908	1,245.75
Towing path embankment, Massillon	W.M. Brode & Son	05/11/1909	2,253.27
Lock 5A S (repair)	W.H. Vogt & Son	06/23/1908	843.51
Retaining wall between Locks 5 and 5A	T.H. Watson & Son	09/??/1909	2,588.83
Lock 5A S and culvert (new)	W.M. Brode & Co.	05/11/1909	7,376.87
Sluice between Locks 5A and 6S	Dailey Bros.	03/13/1907	577.96
Waste way between Locks 5A and 6S	Dailey Bros.	03/13, 1907	145.37
Lock 6S	Dailey Bros.	03/13/1907	5,875.12
Sluice between Locks 6 and 7S	Dailey Bros.	03/13/1907	811.38
Waste way between Locks 6 and 7S	W.H. Vogt & Son	06/23/1908	709.79
Waste way between Locks 6 and 7S	W.H. Vogt & Son	06/23/1908	678.97
Culvert between Locks 6 and 7S	State Forces	1907	207.34
Sluice at Lock 7S	Dailey Bros.	03/13/1907	538.91
Lock 7S	Dailey Bros.	03/13/1907	5,994.71
Lock 8S	Dailey Bros.	03/13/1907	5,725.25
Culvert between Locks 8 and 9S	Dailey Bros.	06/23/1908	3,185.22
Lock 9S	Dailey Bros.	03/13/1907	5,115.35
Lock 10S	Dailey Bros.	03/13/1907	4,636.79

Description	Contractor	Date	Cost
Dredging Zoar to Canal Dover	Edward Bodette	05/11/1909	7,216.82
Zoar dam and regulator, incl. levee	Dailey Bros.	06/23/1908	11,212.21
Waste way between Locks 10 and 11S	Dailey Bros.	03/13/1907	332.07
Sluice between Locks 10 and 11S	Fauver & Renick	03/13/1907	556.25
Sluice between Locks 10 and 11S	Fauver & Renick	03/13/1907	521.35
Lock 11 S	Fauver & Renick	03/13/1907	4,951.77
Waste way between Locks 11 and 12S	Fauver & Renick	03/13/1907	1,633.86
Lock 12 S	Fauver & Renick	03/13/1907	5,468.70
Waste way between Locks 12 and 13S	A. Clark	05/11/1909	1,633.86
Sugar Creek dam and sluice	Clark & Medly	10/13/1908	5,761.71
Dredging, Canal Dover, Tuscarawas	J. Kisner	05/11/1908	8,238.78
Sluice and sewer between	W.H. Vogt and Son	06/23/1908	2,540.13
Locks 12 and 13S			
Lock 13S	S. W. Parshall	03/13/1907	6,873.89
Waste way between Locks	J. N. Kisner	05/11/1907	875.84
13 and 14S			
Lock 14S	H. Minnich	03/13/1907	5,168.81
Sluice between Locks 14 and 15S	J. N. Kisner	05/11/1907	646.44
Waste way between Locks 14 and 15S	J. N. Kisner	05/11/1907	457.02
Lock 15 S	J. N. Kisner	05/11/1907	6,815.15
Lock 16 S	J. N. Kisner	08/01/1906	9,956.68
Hilton Dam S****	Daley Bros.	06/23/1908	14,074.35
Dredging Walhonding Canal	J. N. Kisner	08/01/1906	22,843.70

Description	Contractor	Date	Cost
Walhonding Dam, wall and Feeder	J. N. Kisner	01/15/1907	39,719.00
Locks 31, 32, and 33, Dresden	Clifton Bros.	11/27/1905	13,899.73

* Special appropriation.
** Superstructure awarded to King Bridge Co. of Cleveland, Feb. 14, 1905, and included in price.
*** Superstructure awarded to Capital Construction Co., Sept. 14, 1908.
**** Including the price of $5,450 for Hilton farm.

Notes

1. Planning and Construction

1. Terry K. Woods, "Ohio's Canals and Its People," a slide show with text presented at the annual meeting of the American Society of Archivists, Cincinnati, Ohio, Oct. 2, 1980.

2. Canal Commissioners' Report (1822) in John Kilbourn, *Public Documents Concerning the Ohio Canals* (Columbus, 1832), 31–51.

3. The Canal Enabling Act of February 1825 named this canal between Lake Erie and the Ohio River the Ohio Canal. A legislative act of March 14, 1849, changed the name of the Miami Canal, Miami Extension Canal, and a portion of the Wabash & Erie Canal to the Miami & Erie Canal and also changed the name of the Ohio Canal to the Ohio & Erie Canal. Official documents continued to refer to this waterway as the Ohio Canal throughout its life. Historians currently use both names interchangeably. In this book, I will do the same.

4. Terry K. Woods, "An Introduction," *Towpaths* 13 (1975): 1–15.

5. Jack Gieck, *A Photo Album of Ohio's Canal Era, 1825–1913* (Kent, Ohio: Kent State Univ. Press, 1988), 4.

6. Canal Commissioners' Report (1825) in Kilbourn, *Public Documents,* 176–95; Canal Commissioners' Report (1826), in ibid., 235–50.

7. Isaac Roberdeau, "Mathematics and Treatise on Canals" (1818), p. 7, typescript, Document No. MMC 1649, Library of Congress. Colonel Roberdeau was chief of the U.S. Bureau of Topographical Engineers, War Department, from 1818 to 1829.

8. Noble E. Whitford, *History of the Canal System of the State of New York* (Albany, N.Y.: Brandow Printing Co., 1906), 4.

9. Ronald E. Shaw, *Canals for a Nation: The Canal in the United States, 1790–1860* (Lexington: Univ. Press of Kentucky, 1990), 8. Shaw states that the Erie's dimensions were patterned after those of the Middlesex Canal. However, the Middlesex was used as an example of good organization and management; the dimensions of the Erie Canal belonged to its engineers alone.

10. Harry N. Scheiber, *Ohio Canal Era: A Case Study of Government and the Economy, 1820–1861* (Athens: Ohio Univ. Press, 1969), 47.

11. Roberdeau, "Mathematics and Treatise on Canals," 9.

12. James Emmitt, "Early Pike County," *Chillicothe Leader,* 1886. This description could have been applied to nearly every river valley along the canal's route.

13. Chester A. Finn, "The Ohio Canals: Public Enterprise on the Frontier," *Ohio History* 51 (Jan./Mar. 1942).

14. Terry K. Woods, "The Canal Comes to Cleveland," *American Canals* 34 (Spring 2005): 12. There were 109 sections let from the Summit Pond to Newburg, seven in the extension to Cleveland, and two at the river connection for a total of 118.

15. Ernest Ludlow Bogart, *Internal Improvements and State Debt in Ohio: An Essay in Economic History* (New York: Longmans, Green and Co., 1924), 23.

16. N. N. Hill Jr., *History of Licking County, Ohio: Its Past and Present* (Newark, Ohio: A. A. Graham & Co., 1881), 207.

17. Ernest M. Teagarden, "Builders of the Ohio Canal," *Inland Seas* 19 (1963): 101.

18. J. F. Everhart, *History of Muskingum County, Ohio, with Illustrations and Biographical Sketches of Prominent Men and Pioneers* (Columbus, Ohio: J. F. Everhart & Co., 1882), 206.

19. Bogart, *Internal Improvements and State Debt in Ohio,* 25.

20. C. C. Huntington, *History of the Ohio Canals: Their Construction, Cost, Use and Partial Abandonment* (Columbus: Ohio State Archaeological and Historical Society, 1905), 24–25.

21. Teagarden, "Builders of the Ohio Canal," 99–100.

22. Finn, "The Ohio Canals," 16; Huntington, *History of the Ohio Canals,* 24.

23. Canal Commissioners' Report (1826) in Kilbourn, *Public Documents,* 238.

24. Hill, *History of Licking County,* 215.

25. Ibid., 217.

26. Huntington, *History of the Ohio Canals,* 25.

2. Early Operation

1. Canal Commissioners' Report (1827) in Kilbourn, *Public Documents,* 275.

2. Woods, "The Canal Comes to Cleveland," 13.

3. Samuel P. Orth, *A History of Cleveland, Ohio* (Cleveland: S. J. Clarke Publishing Co., 1910), 696.

4. *Cleveland Herald,* July 13, 1827; Terry K. Woods, *The Ohio & Erie Canal in Stark County* (Massillon, Ohio: The Massillon Museum, 2003).

5. Everhart, *History of Muskingum County,* 479; John H. Hall, *Historical Collections of Coshocton County, Ohio* (Cincinnati: R. Clarke & Co., 1876), 57–59; David Meyer, "The Ohio Canal in Lockport and Newark," *Towpaths* 42 (2004): 49. Oddly enough, the histories of Licking County are silent on any opening ceremonies that may have been held in Newark. Cleveland papers were expecting communication with Newark as early as May 1830, but it appears that the first craft from the lake to Newark did not arrive until July 1830, and then troubles with the Walhonding Feeder and Aqueduct made through traffic unreliable.

6. Aaron R. Van Cleaf, *History of Pickaway County, Ohio, and Representative Citizens* (Evansville, Ind.: Unigraphic, 1978), 212–13.

7. William Alexander Taylor, *Centennial History of Columbus and Franklin County, Ohio* (Chicago: S. J. Clarke Publishing Co., 1909), 59–60.

8. B. F. Sproat, "The Canal," *Scioto Gazette,* Jan. 23, 1911, 6–7.

9. Scheiber, *Ohio Canal Era*, 52.

10. Ben Hayes, "Those Wonderful Ohio Canals," *Columbus Citizen-Journal*, Apr. 2, 1956.

11. Ibid.; Nelson W. Evans, *A History of Scioto County, Ohio, Together with a Pioneer of Southern Ohio* (Portsmouth, Ohio: N. W. Evans, 1903), 335. Evans states that the celebration in Waverly took place Sept. 15, 1832, and that the canal was completed to Portsmouth on Dec. 1.

12. Hayes, *Columbus Citizen-Journal*, Apr. 2, 1956.

13. The author culled the names of more than 27 canal boat lines from newspapers and shipping contracts. Many more short-lived lines likely existed, although some may have been alternate names or partners to existing lines.

14. Scheiber, *Ohio Canal Era*, 245; Hilda Dischinger Morhart, *The Zoar Story* (Dover, Ohio: Seibert Printing Co., 1969), 77.

15. The Board of Public Works Report (1837), Ohio Historical Society (hereafter OHS), and the *Cleveland Herald* (Mar. 2, 1837) mention the initiation of a through line of express packets. Cleveland papers during the mid-1830s detailed the amount of time boats took to reach various ports, and "Agreement Between Four Canal Boat Lines," *Cleveland Herald* (Jan. 24, 1835), details the workings of the principal canal companies. Terry K. Woods, "Canal Boat Types on the Ohio & Erie," *American Canals* 18 (Feb. 1989): 9. Samuel A. Lane, *Fifty Years and Over of Akron and Summit County*, (Akron, Ohio: Beacon Job Dept., 1892), 656, details the status of a line boat captain in the 1840s.

16. Terry K. Woods, "Canal Operation: Collection of Tolls of the Ohio & Erie Canal," *American Canals* 34 (Winter 2005): 7–9; Sproat, "The Canal," 12–13. According to Sproat, "A freight boat's crew generally consisted of a Captain, two steersmen, one bowman, two drivers and a cook. A packet's crew consisted of a Captain, two steersmen, two bowmen, a cook and a steward." Pearl Robert Nye, "Take a Trip on the Canal" (1939), 141–42, unpublished manuscript, Archival Department, University of Akron.

17. Scheiber, *Ohio Canal Era*, 235. The Board of Public Works Reports for 1838 and 1839 itemize the expenditures for lock houses, while the 1860 report cites the legislative act that eliminated the need for lock tenders, except those at feeder gates.

18. Sproat, "The Canal," 13; Franz Anton Ritter von Gerstner, *Early American Railroads* (Stanford, Calif.: Stanford Univ. Press, 1997), 390–91.

19. Scheiber, *Ohio Canal Era*, 245; Canal Commissioners' Report (1837), OHS.

20. *Cleveland Herald*, Mar. 2, 1837; Board of Public Works Reports (1838, 1839, 1860), OHS.

21. Huntington, *History of the Ohio Canals*, 35–41.

22. Bogart, *Internal Improvements*, 49–50.

23. Lane, *Fifty Years*, 66–68.

24. Bogart, *Internal Improvements*, 90.

25. Shaw, *Canals for a Nation*, 127–28, outlines the route of the Ohio Canal from lake to river. Frank W. Trevorrow, in *The Water Supply of Ohio's Canals* (Privately published, 1975), outlines the deficiencies over the years of the water supply at both Ohio Canal summits as well as the need to continually enlarge the reservoirs.

26. Bogart, *Internal Improvements*, 89.

27. Scheiber, *Ohio Canal Era*, 216–17.

28. Terry K. Woods, "Over Ohio Hills in a Canal Boat," *The Gamut* 25 (Winter 1988): 80.

29. Board of Public Works Report (1843) describes the changes made in canal boat shape and design.

30. Annals of Cleveland: A Depression-Era Project of the WPA. In 1846, mentions of coal began appearing in Cleveland newspaper articles as an important incoming cargo and was a significant item by 1848. Woods, "Canal Boat Types on the Ohio & Erie," 7–8.

31. Huntington, *History of the Ohio Canals*, 170–71.

32. Bogart, *Internal Improvements*, 177.

33. Canal Commissioners' Report (1844), OHS. A great deal of the building stone originally used on the canal sections below Lancaster deteriorated quickly. Many locks and other stone structures in the area had to be rebuilt in the 1840s.

34. Scheiber, *Ohio Canal Era*, 176–77.

35. Ibid., 287–88.

36. Ibid., 245.

37. Bogart, *Internal Improvements*, 101–2.

38. Scheiber, *Ohio Canal Era*, 298–99.

39. Bogart, *Internal Improvements*, 105–7.

40. *Cleveland Leader*, Jan. 26, 1860.

41. Bogart, *Internal Improvements*, 109.

42. Scheiber, *Ohio Canal Era*, 305–6.

3. Administration and Finance

1. Scheiber, *Ohio Canal Era*, 36–37. The first members of the Canal Fund Board were the former governor Ethan Allen Brown, often called the "father of Ohio's canals"; Ebenezer Buckingham, previously a canal commissioner and one of the wealthiest businessmen in the state; and future governor Allen Trimble. Trimble resigned in 1826 to pursue his political career and was replaced by Simon Perkins, an influential banker from Ohio's Western Reserve.

2. Bogart, *Internal Improvements*, 30–31.

3. Scheiber, *Ohio Canal Era*, 61–62. The position of principal engineer was eliminated after 1829.

4. Ibid., 65–66.

5. Ibid., 67–68.

6. "Claim State Canal Lands Should Belong to Farmers," *Dover Daily Reporter*, Apr. 9, 1913.

7. Terry K. Woods, ed., "The Miami Extension Canal," *Towpaths* 13 (1975): 19–22; "The Dresden Sidecut," ibid., 58.

8. Scheiber, *Ohio Canal Era*, 166–68.

9. Bogart, *Internal Improvements*, 56–57.

10. Huntington, *History of the Ohio Canals*, 63–65.

11. Bogart, *Internal Improvements*, 40–41.

12. Ibid., 35, 37, 46.

13. Ibid., 31–32.

14. Scheiber, *Ohio Canal Era*, 168–69.

15. Ibid., 176–77.

16. Huntington, *History of the Ohio Canals*, 31–32. By January 1832, the cost of the Ohio Canal was more than $1 million over the 1825 estimate.

17. Bogart, *Internal Improvements*, 60–65.

18. Ibid., 66–67.

19. Ibid., 70–72.

20. Ibid., 75–77. At the time, state auditors could not determine the exact cost of Ohio's canals. In 1924, Bogart estimated that the main Ohio Canal had cost $4,695,204; the Walhonding Canal $607,269; the Hocking Canal $975,481; and the Muskingum Improvement $1,628,028.

21. Board of Public Works Report (1864), OHS; Akron, Cleveland, and Cincinnati newspapers of the period.

22. Bogart, *Internal Improvements,* 115–16.

23. Ibid., 132–34.

24. Ibid., 136–38.

25. Ibid., 134–35.

26. Board of Public Works Report (1912), OHS.

4. Operation of the Lease

1. "Investigation Concerning the Public Works of Ohio" (Columbus, Ohio: Nevins and Meyers, 1875), testimony of A. B. Newburgh, secretary, Ohio State Board of Public Works, Jan. 16, 1875, p. 6, and testimony of Samuel Doyle, Jan. 21, 1875, p. 33.

2. *Akron Beacon Journal,* June 13, 1861, 3.

3. Board of Public Works Report (1864), OHS; *Akron Beacon Journal,* Jan. 7, 1874. There are a number of these acts on record. The *Beacon Journal* reprinted an article from the *Cincinnati Commercial* decidedly uncomplimentary toward the lessees.

4. Board of Public Works Reports (1864, 1876, 1878), OHS.

5. "Investigation Concerning the Public Works of Ohio," testimony of Thomas West, 113. Lock 12 in Tuscarawas County was repaired in this manner prior to 1870.

6. Board of Public Works Report (1876), OHS.

7. *Akron Beacon Journal,* Jan. 8, 1863.

8. Scheiber, *Ohio Canal Era,* 166–68.

9. "Investigation Concerning the Public Works of Ohio," testimonies of Newburgh and Doyle.

10. Boatmen and citizens living along the canal, taped interviews with author, Dec. 1969 to Jan. 1990.

11. *Akron Beacon Journal,* July 12, 1872; ibid., July 16, 1872.

12. Bogart, *Internal Improvements,* 122–26.

13. Cleveland papers of 1873 note that the city of Cleveland paid $125,000 for this section of the canal to the lessees, not the state. The state sued the city over this land years later but never received a cent.

14. Huntington, *History of the Ohio Canals,* 48–49; Terry K. Woods, "Outlet Lock at Cleveland, 1875," *American Canals* 19 (Aug. 1990): 8. Though most accounts date the closing of the Cleveland terminus to 1873, required construction of new terminal facilities below Dille Street at the southern city limits meant that the original terminus was in use through the 1877 boating season.

15. John R. Grabb, *The Canal: Its Rise and Fall in Ross County: Seventy-five Years of Canal Transportation in Southern Ohio and Its Effect on the Economy* (Chillicothe, Ohio: Ross County Historical Society, 1985), 6.

16. "Investigation Concerning the Public Works of Ohio," testimony of Doyle.

17. Bogart, *Internal Improvements,* 127. Bogart refers to the Board of Public Works Report for 1879.

18. Ibid., 115. I believe that the closing of the original northern canal terminus in Cleveland near the end of the 1877 boating season was more than coincidental to the abandonment of the lease.

19. Board of Public Works Reports (1878, 1879), OHS.

20. Board of Public Works Reports (1878, 1879), OHS; Bogart, *Internal Improvements,* 128.

21. Bogart, *Internal Improvements,* 118.

22. Woods, "Canal Boat Types on the Ohio & Erie," 8–9.

23. Frank W. Trevorrow, "The Federal Surveys of Ohio's Canals," *Towpaths* 25 (1987): 44–46.

24. Bogart, *Internal Improvements,* 117.

25. Ibid., 30–32.

26. Trevorrow, "The Federal Surveys of Ohio's Canals," 52–53.

27. Board of Public Works Report (1902), OHS.

28. Author interviews with boatmen in the 1960s, 1970s, and 1980s indicate that boating on the northern section of the Ohio Canal was not easy during the last few years of the nineteenth century or the early twentieth century. Woods, *The Ohio & Erie Canal in Stark County,* 24.

29. Board of Public Works Report (1903), OHS.

30. Board of Public Works Report (1903), OHS; "The Future of the Canals," *Cleveland Leader,* Mar. 22, 1904.

31. Terry K. Woods, *Twenty-five Miles to Nowhere* (Coshocton, Ohio: Roscoe Village Foundation, 1991), 47–48.

32. Frank Trevorrow, "Ohio's Canals: The Final Years," *Towpaths* 28 (1990): 5.

33. "The Ohio Canal," *The Roller Monthly,* 1901; *New Philadelphia Daily Times,* Mar. 15, 1907.

34. Author interviews with former boatmen in the 1960s, 1970s, and 1980s.

35. Board of Public Works Reports (1906, 1907, 1908, 1909), OHS. Taped interviews with Waldo Streby, 1988 and 1990, tell of the activity in the canal around Summit Lake.

36. Trevorrow, "Ohio's Canals," 8–9.

37. Board of Public Works Reports (1909, 1911), OHS.

5. The Flood

1. Board of Public Works Report (1911), OHS. It appears that state forces removed the Walhonding Aqueduct sometime between the engineers' reports of 1909 and 1911.

2. Edith McNally, author interview, 1978. Dillow Robinson recalled the need to haul cargo from Cleveland to Akron by canal. However, no boats were active, and an old houseboat had to be dragged off the bank and pressed into use. Two men working hand pumps kept the old, dried-up hulk from sinking to the bottom of the canal before they reached Akron.

3. Board of Public Works Reports (1912, 1913), OHS; interviews with Silvia Klingler in 1972 and Dillow Robinson in the 1970s and 1980s. Silvia was aboard a cook boat for the dredge crew from Barberton to Massillon during the 1907 to 1909 seasons, and Robinson was a member of the state boat crew that leveled off the canal towpath in Canal Fulton in 1912.

4. Board of Public Works Reports (1911, 1912), OHS.

5. George W. Knepper, *Ohio and Its People* (Kent, Ohio: Kent State Univ. Press, 1997), 140

6. John McLaughlin (son of Canal Fulton dry dock owner Charles McLaughlin), author interview, Mar. 1972.

7. "Old Pictures Recall Great Flood Disaster That Inundated Massillon 21 Years Ago," *Massillon Independent,* Mar. 1934; Ruth Kane, "1913 Flood Was Worst in History of Massillon," *Massillon Independent,* Mar. 26, 1976.

8. Ohio Historical Society, "March 23–27, 1913: Statewide Flood," www.ohiohistory. org/etcetera/exhibits/swio/pages/content/1913_flood.htm (accessed Apr. 8, 2008); local

newspaper accounts of the flood from Cleveland, Akron, Massillon, New Philadelphia-Dover, and Coshocton.

9. Larry Neely, "City Battered by Devastating Flood," *Massillon Independent,* Mar. 23, 1963.

10. Gieck, *Photo Album of Ohio's Canal Era,* 280–82; taped interview with John Henry Vance by Jack Gieck; Ted Dettling, "The Day They Blew Up Lock 8," *Towpaths* 11 (1973): 34.

11. Ohio Historical Society Web site, "March 23–27, 1913: Statewide Flood."

12. Dillow Robinson, author interview, Apr. 12, 1972. Robinson turned 14 a few days prior to the 1913 flood.

13. "Severe Weather in Ohio," Ohio Historical Society, www.ohiohistory.org/etcetera/exhibits/swio/# (accessed Mar. 5, 2008).

14. *The New Philadelphia Daily Times,* 1913, declared the canal irreparable; *Dover Daily Reporter,* Mar. 26, 1913.

15. Board of Public Works Report (1913), OHS.

16. "Canal Fulton Man Supervises Old Canal," *Canton Repository,* Mar. 12, 1927.

17. Terry K. Woods, "The Roscoe Hydraulic Plant," *American Canals* 7 (Summer 2001): 5–6.

18. Herbert T. O. Blue, *History of Stark County, Ohio, from the Age of Prehistoric Man to the Present Day* (Chicago: S. J. Clark Pub. Co., 1928), 347–49. The twin culverts are still in the wall of the McClain warehouse building in Massillon, though many layers of asphalt on Charles Street SW have covered all but the top courses of the western structure.

19. Conversations with Bill Wallace, director of the Summit County Historical Society, and Ted Dettling, Board of the Summit County Historical Society, early 1970s. The *Akron Beacon Journal,* Dec. 4, 1961, mentions that the businesses over the canal were being razed for city improvements.

20. Dillow Robinson, interview by Edith McNally, Oct. 24, 1978.

21. Waldo Streby, author interview, Jan. 2, 1990. Streby grew up in Canal Fulton and was a playmate of Billy McGee, Johnny Moore's grandson. During the flu epidemic of 1918, when all the schools were closed, Johnny Moore, the local canal maintenance supervisor, hired a number of boys, including McGee and Streby, to work on refurbishing the canal as far south as Navarre.

22. "Canal Land Purchase by City Is Approved," *Massillon Independent,* June 23, 1949.

23. Ibid.

24. Burton P. Porter, *Old Canal Days* (Columbus, Ohio: Heer Printing Co., 1942), 7.

25. Conservation Bulletin, Sept. 1938, Ohio Department of Natural Resources.

26. Woods, *The Ohio & Erie Canal in Stark County,* 25.

27. "Canal Land Purchase by City Is Approved," June 23, 1949.

28. Ron Gray, director of the Akron's Ohio Division of Water, telephone conversation with the author, Mar. 17, 2006.

29. "State of Ohio Dept. of Public Works & Columbus, Ohio, Study and Report on Improvements to the Ohio & Erie Canal," *The Barnes Report,* Apr. 15, 1952. A photo collection at the Akron Public Library details the 1951 storm sewer project, and Akron newspaper clippings from 1963 laud the downtown improvement.

30. Ohio Department of Natural Resources, Division of Water, "Portage Lakes Water Supply," www.dnr.state.oh.us/water/pubs/fs_div/fctsht04/tabid/4084/default.aspx (accessed May 2, 2008).

31. Unidentified "Sunday supplement" newspaper clipping, probably a Cleveland paper from 1935, Massillon Public Library; Aaron J. Keirns, *Black Hand Gorge: A Journey Through Time* (Howard, Ohio: Little River Publishing Co., 1995), 77, 108.

32. David Meyer, email to author, July 30, 2007.

6. Effects of the Canal

1. Huntington, *History of the Ohio Canals*, 110; A. R. Johnson, "Ohio Canal Systems Historical Data," (Columbus: Ohio Division of Public Works, 1968). This analysis of Ohio's canals determined that they actually earned $5,219,487.71. More conventional accounting practices found the canals suffered an overall loss of $14,780,513.29.

2. Scheiber, *Ohio Canal Era*, 9–11.

3. Oliver Jensen, *The American Heritage History of Railroads in America* (New York: American Heritage/Wings Books, 1993), 34. By 1840, 3,000 miles of track had been laid, and this grew to more than 9,000 miles by 1850.

4. Knepper, *Ohio and its People*, 131. Initially, Ohio ranked third behind New York and Pennsylvania; now Ohio is third behind California and Texas, according to www.real-estate-2000.com/ohio.htm (accessed Mar. 5, 2008).

5. Scheiber, *Ohio Canal Era*, 189, 192.

6. Gieck, *Photo Album of Ohio's Canal Era*, 264–65.

7. Librarian at Ramsayer Library, Stark County Historical Society, email to author, Jan. 6, 2006.

8. Huntington, *History of the Ohio Canals*, 132–34.

9. Of the 27 canal passenger and freight line names gathered by the author, seven operated the entire length of both the Erie and Ohio Canals.

10. Peninsula and Canal Fulton are part of the federally mandated Ohio & Erie Canal Heritage Corridor. Roscoe Village is the beneficiary of a private endowment, the Montgomery Foundation.

11. An 1854 painting, housed at the Massillon Museum, depicts the Kent Jarvis estate, with its manicured lawn and lavish fountains, on the bank of the canal south of Massillon's lower lock.

12. Woods, "The Ohio & Erie Canal in Stark County," 30. Italy Hill, or "Dago Hill," was a beautifully terraced embankment on the Ohio & Erie Canal on the south side of Navarre and reflected the handiwork of the Italian immigrant mine workers who lived there. Pearl Robert Nye, "Take a Trip on the Ohio Canal" (1993), ed. Terry K. Woods, *Towpaths* 31 (1993): 35. Nye mentions "Black Dog Crossing," which was a euphemism for the area in the 1880s.

13. Ben and Wick Ludenberger, interviews with author, Nov. 1971 and Jan. 1972.

14. Nye, "Take a Trip on the Ohio Canal." Nye's father had 18 children by two wives, highlighting the clannish connection.

15. Ibid. Throughout the manuscript, Nye makes known his feelings of superiority over the "Town Jakes."

16. "The Canal," *Roller Monthly*, 1901.

17. Terry K. Woods, "The Last Girl Baby Born on the Ohio Canal," *American Canals* 34 (Fall 2005): 7. The last girl born on the canal was delivered on her parents' boat, which was anchored below Lock 1 in Akron in 1929. Pearl Nye was her uncle.

18. That seems to have been a male emotion. With few exceptions, the female boatmen (they were called boatmen too) were happy to get off the canal, and most never wanted to go back.

Recommended Reading

Bogart, Ernest Ludlow. *Internal Improvements and State Debt in Ohio: An Essay in Economic History.* New York: Longmans, Green and Co., 1924. This is probably the most historically accurate treatment of Ohio's canal era, particularly the account of the financial manipulations of various state entities as the canals were being built and operated. Unfortunately, this book has been out of print for many years and is slowly disappearing from library shelves.

Gieck, Jack E. *A Photo Album of Ohio's Canal Era, 1825–1913.* Kent, Ohio: Kent State University Press, 1988. Widely considered the bible on Ohio's canals, this book is a photo album rather than a detailed history. It covers all the major Ohio canals and has terrific photos. There are a few historical inaccuracies, and a small number of the photos are incorrectly identified, but it is, overall, an excellent and entertaining reference book.

Huntington, C. C., and C. P. McClelland. *History of the Ohio Canals: Their Construction, Cost, Use and Partial Abandonment.* Columbus: Ohio State Archaeological and Historical Society, 1905. This Ohio State University graduate project contains a number of historical inaccuracies, but, as one of the earliest efforts to document the history of Ohio's canal era, it ranks as one of the better ones.

Scheiber, Harry N. *Ohio Canal Era: A Case Study of Government and the Economy, 1820–1861.* Athens: Ohio University Press, 1969. This is an excellent scholarly work on Ohio's canals, though it stops short of the lease period. The book has a few historical inaccuracies, but it is generally extremely well researched and presented.

Wilcox, Frank N. *The Ohio Canals.* Kent, Ohio: Kent State University Press, 1969. This is primarily a showcase for Wilcox's wonderful canal drawings and paintings. The text that accompanies the artwork was taken from Wilcox's hiking notes after his death. As a result, there are a considerable number of historical inaccuracies. However, the artwork is an extremely accurate representation of the canal structures, making this book a valuable tool.

Index